WHEN A BABY DIES

WHEN A BABY DIES

Jill Worth

Hodder & Stoughton

A MEMBER OF THE HODDER HEADLINE GROUP

First published in Great Britain in 1995
by Hodder and Stoughton.

10 9 8 7 6 5 4 3 2 1

British Library Cataloguing in Publication Data
A record for this book is available from the British Library

ISBN 0 340 62176 1

Typeset by Phoenix Typesetting, Ilkley, West Yorkshire.

Printed and bound in Great Britain by
Cox & Wyman Ltd, Reading, Berkshire.

Hodder and Stoughton Ltd
A division of Hodder Headline PLC
338 Euston Road
London NW1 3BH

In memory of
Felicity Jane,
whose short life caused this book to be written

Contents

Preface

How do grieving parents learn to live without their beloved children? What is the answer when they question, 'Why?' Or when they ask, 'Where is God in this?'

All the couples whose stories are told in these pages have asked those questions. Their babies have died – some through miscarriage or stillbirth. Others have suffered cot death or heart defect, or have been unable to survive their premature birth.

Unlike other books on bereavement, you won't find in these pages conclusions, summing-up, or spiritual advice from the author. Each chapter stands alone as a 'testimony' of grief. Men and women have been free to tell their own story of their spiritual and emotional journey through grief. Free to say, to anyone who will listen, '*This is how it feels to lose a baby.*'

They talk about what has helped them, and what has hindered their journey. How they feel friends, family and the church have supported them – or let them down. How their experience has changed them as individuals, and changed their relationship with each other – and with God.

There are no 'miracles' here. No stories of babies who appeared to have died but were miraculously alive again. Yet the stories are miracles – miracles of parents rebuilding shattered lives.

I would like to offer my grateful thanks to all the couples who so openly and honestly shared their personal experiences. And, with them, I hope that their honesty will help others.

I

Her name was Alice

Mary and John had been married for two and a half years. It was Mary's second marriage; she was divorced from her first husband, and already had three sons. The two older boys lived with their father, but the youngest, twelve-year-old Daniel, lived with Mary and John.

Mary had been sterilised in her twenties, but when she and John decided they wanted a child of their own, they visited the doctor to discuss sterilisation reversal. The day before her thirty-seventh birthday, Mary went to hospital to have the reversal operation.

Nine months later, in February 1986, Mary knew she was pregnant. John remembers coming home from work and finding Mary in the kitchen. She had a cough, and John told her to take some medicine, but she kept on refusing. At first annoyed that she wouldn't do something so simple to relieve the cough, he eventually asked himself why she was unwilling to take any medication. The penny dropped. 'You're not, are you?' he asked her.

'We were so delighted, so happy,' John recalls. But the couple, hardly daring to believe it was true, put off doing a pregnancy test for another two weeks. Yet once they plucked up the courage to do the test together at home, it was confirmed. Mary was pregnant.

'We couldn't believe it!' says Mary. 'I started looking at baby things in the shops straight away.'

The next day they had lunch with John's parents, and told them the good news. John's grandmother was invited to lunch, and heard she was going to be a great-grandmother.

But two weeks after the test, Mary started to bleed. Then the pains started. By the time John arrived home from work, the pregnancy was over.

John remembers coming home to find Mary lying on the bed, telling him simply, 'I'm losing the baby.' John phoned Mary's sister, who was a nurse, to describe what was happening and ask, 'What do we do?' She told him, 'Mary's having a miscarriage, there's nothing you can do. It just happens.'

'We lay on the bed and didn't say anything,' remembers John. 'There was just nothing. We hadn't learnt to express our emotions, or to trust each other.'

They were supposed to be going to homegroup that night. They discussed whether they should go or not, and initially decided they shouldn't, as they must give themselves time to grieve. But then they changed their minds. Although this had happened to them, they decided, life must go on.

'So we went to homegroup,' says John. 'We usually participated, but on that occasion we said absolutely nothing for the whole evening, and no one said anything to us.'

'We had no one to tell,' he says. 'It was just the two of us, lost and alone. We were stunned. There was no one outside the situation we could talk and pray with. There are people we could do that with now, but there weren't then. So we just muddled through ourselves, until we eventually found out that it had to be worked through, and we had to talk and pray about it. But that wasn't until much later.'

John's family hadn't reacted much when they heard of the pregnancy, and he recalls they said something along the lines of 'too bad' when they heard of the miscarriage. John himself had been brought up to hide his emotions, and this had a devastating effect on his reaction to his baby's death, and his relationship with Mary. Not only was he unable to talk to her about how he felt, but he couldn't admit his feelings to himself either.

So when John agreed with Mary's suggestion that they should try for another baby quite soon, he wasn't admitting his true feelings, and he wasn't being truthful. 'I actually didn't want to try again, because of the pain of losing it,' he said. 'But Mary did, so I said I did too.

'I didn't want to think about it at all. But I couldn't say so, because we weren't communicating. Looking back from where we are now, I'd say yes, I do want to try. But I couldn't tell her how I was feeling inside then.

'I didn't allow myself to feel much. But when anyone mentioned babies I'd cry, thinking about our baby, although it wasn't often, and it was always on my own. As the weeks went by, I told myself, "This has gone on long enough, it's not as if it was a real baby, it wasn't alive." Mary grieved, but I kept it inside for a long time. It wasn't until years later that I was forced to face up to it, as part of healing for all kinds of things, and I was devastated by it, because I realised that a child was what I really wanted.

'We didn't make love that often, and we were ill or tired or cross whenever it was the best time to conceive,' John says. 'I felt under pressure to make the effort to produce another baby. Mary tried to provoke me, saying things like "Nobody's ever going to call you Dad," to make me face up to what I felt.'

'I pressurised John because I desperately wanted another baby,' says Mary. 'But he seemed to be backing off all the time. He always seemed to be out, or too tired, at *the* times of the month. I felt so angry with him. But we didn't talk about it.

'Our home became a battleground. I was getting so upset, and shouting so often. Everything was deteriorating.'

It was only years later that John told her, 'I always felt you wanted to take a child from me, not give love to me.' Mary says she was taken aback to know John had felt like that. 'I realised that he'd felt I didn't care about him any more, but didn't know why,' she says.

Mary, too, was unable to face up to her grief immediately. 'I didn't talk about it for a month,' she says. 'I pretended it hadn't happened, and behaved as usual.' It wasn't until she found out her sister was pregnant with her second child that the tears started.

When the couple had been round the shops looking at baby things, they had actually put some money down on a pram. 'But we never went back for the refund – we couldn't bear it,' says John.

Mary saw a counsellor from the church twice, but it didn't help. Neither did she feel supported by the church – although she admits not many people knew she had been pregnant, so they couldn't have been expected to ask how she was coping.

The reaction among those who did know was often, 'Oh well, at least you know the operation worked, and you can still have another one.' But Mary didn't want another one, she wanted the baby she'd lost.

When she heard that her sister's baby might be born early, Mary had an awful fear that it would come on the day her own baby had been due. But the baby, Michael, was born on time. Even so, she couldn't go to see her nephew when he was born. And when she did pluck up the courage to visit, about three weeks later, she didn't want to hold him.

That Christmas, when Michael was six weeks old, he contracted meningitis. Although he was desperately ill, Mary felt unable to visit either him or her sister. Her father was surprised at her reaction, because it was so out of character. He said to her afterwards, 'Michael nearly died – didn't you realise how serious it was?'

'And I felt like screaming at him, "Michael *nearly* died – but my baby *really* died," ' says Mary. 'But it was forgotten. After I'd first told them about it, my parents had never referred to my miscarriage again.

'If you've given birth to a baby, people think it's more serious when it dies. Michael was a live baby who nearly died. But they dismiss miscarriage – and *early* miscarriage in particular.'

Mary's son Daniel was quite relieved to hear there wasn't going to be a baby. Mary found out later that he had been worried that John, his step-father, wouldn't love him once he had a child of his own. 'I could understand where he was coming from,' says Mary.

First the months, and then the years, went by, and Mary did not become pregnant again. 'Those months and months of waiting for another child!' exclaims Mary. 'The tears, the pain, the heartache every month – and the quarrels that resulted!

'Eventually I had to come to terms with the fact that there wasn't going to be another baby,' she says. 'Looking back, I think it was the last straw. I'd managed to fail in pretty well every area of my life, and now I couldn't even have John's child.

'I felt I'd let John down. He had no children of his own, and he'd taken on one of mine. He was younger than me, and I had this feeling that he'd get to forty and say he wanted children – and I couldn't have any. I was fearful he'd reject me if I didn't have a child.

'And I was letting his family down, too. His parents would never have grandchildren, his grandmother would never have a great-grandchild.

'It seemed that everybody else was having children. I felt so angry with God. I felt he was cheating on me. He kept taking things away from me. It might not be what the Bible said, but I felt it was what was happening to me. I'd been married, and then divorced. I'd had three children, but two of them weren't living with me. And now I'd lost John's baby.'

A great deal of Mary's anger stemmed from the circumstances behind the pregnancy. 'Right from the beginning we prayed that if God didn't want us to have a child, the whole process of the sterilisation reversal wouldn't work,' says Mary. 'We prayed at each stage, "Don't let it get this far unless there's going to be a baby." '

The couple had been to a top London hospital to make sure the sterilisation could be reversed. First, Mary had a laparoscopy to find whether she had enough tube left to make the reversal even a possibility. They prayed: 'If there's not going to be a child, then let the answer be no.' But the answer was yes – it was fine to go ahead.

Then John's sperm was tested – since without John's fertility being positively established, it would be pointless for Mary to have the reversal operation. Again they prayed: 'If there's not going to be a child, let John be infertile.' Again, the result was positive.

And when the operation to reverse the sterilisation was carried out, they prayed that prayer again: 'Let the operation be a failure, if there's not going to be a child.' But the operation was a success. The doctor's last words were, 'I look forward to hearing the good news when it happens.'

And finally Mary prayed: 'Let me not get pregnant unless there's going to be a child for us to bring up.'

'So when we lost the baby, that was the biggest difficulty, the biggest question mark,' says Mary. 'I had to say to God, "Why didn't you stop it at the beginning? Why did you let me get pregnant and then take it away?" It was like having a carrot dangled in front of me, then snatched away. So the question was not so much "Why me?" but "Why did you let it get this far?" '

Mary blamed herself. Not only did she question whether she'd scrubbed the floor too vigorously, or whether the bath water was too hot, but she would think, 'Maybe I'm such an awful mother that God doesn't think I'm fit to have another child.' Immediately, she would tell herself that God wasn't like that. 'But why didn't what happened to me tie up with what I read in the Bible? I searched and searched for an answer.'

John, too, thought he must be to blame. 'I honestly felt that God thought I wouldn't be a good parent,' he says. 'I wasn't good enough to be a father, so Mary lost the baby.

'You can look back and try to justify it. I tried to rationalise it, to find a reason why it happened. Perhaps it was because Mary and I weren't communicating, so it wouldn't have been good to bring a baby up in those conditions. But that's no answer. No, it wouldn't have been a good place to bring a baby into at that time – but as life's gone on, and our relationship has changed, our home would have been a good place for a child.

'You can say, "Perhaps she would have been handicapped." But that's not an answer either. God could have made a baby who *wasn't* handicapped. And even if she was handicapped, we would still have loved her. You see the parents of handicapped children, loving them, and those children have a lot to give.

'I had the feeling – how come Mary has three children and I don't? If her first husband was entitled to three children, why didn't I get any? I felt – right or wrong – that I was better than him. Then I'd start thinking it must have been a mistake to marry Mary. Was God telling us it was a mistake for us to marry, therefore we'll never have children?'

John says he tried to rationalise it because he couldn't cope with it at the time. 'I don't think I was angry for the first few years, but in the end you have to be honest with yourself, and with God. It's only recently I faced up to it, and said to God, "I don't know why you took my baby away." But God didn't answer. And you can be angry with God and say, "I think you've got it wrong."

'There's no point in rationalising it. You can never say, "There's a good reason for this, I accept it." That's man-made faith. True faith is *not* understanding. I don't know why God allows these things. I can't tie up what happened with God and his love.

'In Exodus 33:11, it says, "The Lord used to speak to Moses face to face, as a man speaks to his friend." And that's what you can do, you can tell God you think he's wrong.'

He still doesn't know why it happened. 'You never get an answer,' he says. 'But God still says "Trust me", and you can decide whether or not to trust him. You can say yes, I know whatever happens, you are completely trustworthy. Because God doesn't go round killing babies.

'I had to work out what kind of God he was. I had to ask, "Do you sit there having a laugh at us? Do you say you're good, but really you're malicious? Is it all a big con, a big joke?" I don't think it is now, but I had to ask that then.

'Jesus died for us, he knows how we suffer. He was a man of sorrows, acquainted with grief. You have to trust God enough to say, "This is how I feel, here it is, have this lot." He's big enough to take the pain and the hurt, because that's what he died for.

'Nothing compensates. We have a new lifestyle now, and I'm very grateful. Mary's got a good job, and she really enjoys it. We've got our own house, we've got more money than we had then. But it's not compensation. We can't say we're glad we didn't have a baby because if we had we would have been less well off than we are now, and we wouldn't have been able to buy a new car. God doesn't say, "Sorry about the baby, here's heaps of money instead."

'Neither does it compensate if you are able to help someone else through a similar experience. I don't accept that God says, "I want you to be a help to other people, so I'm going to make your life an absolute misery." Yes, you do get an acceptance and understanding of people, and it helps to be able to help someone else. But it doesn't make up for what happened.

'You never get over it. I still think, I'm never, ever, going to be a father – and I think I'd have been quite a good one.

'It's like that song from *Fiddler on the Roof* – "would it spoil some vast eternal plan" if we'd been allowed to have a baby? Would it really have made such a terrible difference?'

One great comfort to both Mary and John was that they felt they knew what the baby was named. 'It just came to me one day: "This baby's called Alice," ' says Mary. 'At first I told myself not to be so ridiculous. We didn't even know whether it was a girl. But when I told John, he said he felt the same name had been given to him.'

Soon after the miscarriage, Mary started looking after the children of another family in the church. 'I became a mother's help, because I knew that if I didn't spend time with children immediately, I would never be able to touch a child again,' she says.

She eventually sought prayer healing from an organisation called Wholeness Through Christ. 'It resulted in a lot of healing over the years, and it made me realise there was an awful lot in me that I hadn't faced.' John, too, went for healing, and as time went on, they both felt they were being called into prayer ministry.

'We've been through an awful lot in our lives, as well as losing the baby, and we've been through the healing. And now we can say to other people, "Jesus can release you, whether it's from miscarriage, abuse, divorce, rejection or guilt," ' says John.

'It doesn't take away the sense of loss; it doesn't stop you wanting the baby; it doesn't stop you wishing you were a father. But you know you're not alone. Jesus is there with us, and he doesn't take it away, but he's someone you can offload on to, and it makes a difference. It gives peace.'

Mary says there is still a gap in her life. She has three children, but not by the man she loves. 'As life goes on, you don't think about it so much,' she says. 'But when you do, you realise how much it still hurts.

'Yet God can use these things to help other people – and that helps the healing in yourself. I would never have fully understood anyone else's pain if I hadn't been through it. But it was at least three years before I got to the stage where I could think positively like that.

'As I've sorted things out I've grown spiritually, and I'm much more aware that there is evil in the world. God hasn't given me these disasters; he's taken me through them. He wasn't trying to get me – he does love me, unconditionally. And he can bring good out of absolute disaster, even though it doesn't seem like it at the time. I'm much more able to trust God now because of it, in a way that I couldn't before. Yes, it was awful – but I've become so much closer to God.'

2

Anna Ceridwen: 144 days

In 1983, thirty-five-year-old David was ordained as a Methodist minister, and he and his family moved to South Wales. It was with mixed emotions that his wife, Sue, faced this next change in their lives.

In the previous seven years, the family had moved several times. In 1976 they had left North London, where David had worked as an architect, to attend Bible college. After two years, they returned to London, where David had spent three further years as an associate minister. In his third year there, he became a candidate for the Methodist ministry, and the family moved to Cambridge where David took a theology degree.

Sue's mother had died of a stroke in the same week as David's ordination. So yet another move, with three young children, wasn't easy. But Sue found a warm welcome and caring concern, particularly at one of the Methodist churches for which David was responsible, and she became a member there.

In November 1984, Sue found part-time work as a health visitor. 'Financially it was imperative,' she says. 'The children were beginning to request new clothes, not the jumble-sale ones I usually bought! I had always felt called to health visiting or pastoral work, and now Alice, our youngest, was six years old, it was a good time to return to it. It seemed we would not have more children – although we were unwilling to be final about it.'

She loved her work, in a deprived area of South Wales. So she says she was 'stunned' to find herself pregnant in July 1985. But in September, when Sue miscarried the baby at about seven weeks, she and all the family grieved their loss. 'It shook me a good deal,' she admits, 'to realise how common this occurrence was to many families I cared for as a health visitor. I never underestimated the experience and the effect on families after that.'

Sue kept a diary of the four days after the miscarriage, written in hospital, where she had a D&C. Reading it years later, it hit her again that it truly was a disaster to lose a child even at such an early stage.

The following July, the whole family flew to the USA on an exchange visit with an American minister. Returning after seven weeks, on 25 August 1986, Sue started to suspect she was again pregnant.

'We'd used contraceptives and the safe period,' she says, 'so I blamed the climate and travelling for altering my cycle!'

'My pregnancy was probably greeted by a rather frightened me, because of the experience of the miscarriage, and my age,' says Sue. 'However, once I was past the first four months, my feelings were optimistic. I was offered tests, which we refused. I could not have accepted a termination on any grounds.'

The couple both felt more hopeful about the outcome of this pregnancy, and knew this would be their last child. Sue says her pregnancy was uneventful, and she felt fit throughout – even though she was forty years old on 18 October that year. She only had a few minor problems – a spot of blood one day, a scan at four months finding the placenta lying low, which rectified itself, and an acute pain in her abdomen at seven months, although the doctor could find nothing wrong.

She continued to work right up to the eighth month. 'I was sad to leave work, but I didn't want to deny our fourth child the time and energy given to the others in those first crucial years,' says Sue. 'I knew I had plenty of other things to do locally, such as returning to help at a successful mother and toddler group at church, which I had helped to found.'

The baby was due on 20 May. On that day, Sue felt sure she had gone into labour. But after a few hours in hospital in the late evening, when there were hardly any staff on duty, everything quietened down, and she was discharged home.

On the morning of 26 May, Sue felt contractions again. She persisted at home, even taking the dog, Lassie, for a walk to the local park, stopping every so often to breathe through the contractions.

When the pains were coming every five minutes, David and Sue went to the local hospital, only a few minutes away. Arriving there at 2 p.m., Sue insisted she was in advanced labour. But there wasn't a free bed in the labour suite, and she had to sit on a chair in a maternity ward while monitors and a bed were made ready.

After about two hours, Sue told the staff that she was ready to push. Visitors – who were at the bedsides of the other women on the ward – had to be told quickly to leave and the ward cleared so Sue could give birth. Her 8lb 15oz baby girl, Anna Ceridwen, was delivered straight on to the hospital bed with all the screens just pulled around. It was 4.14 p.m. Sue had a listening audience of about six mothers, some of whom had just delivered that morning.

'I was mad that the delivery was so undignified (can it ever be dignified?) and wished I'd remained at home,' says Sue. 'I felt the hospital gave no extras, in safety or comfort, and it may even have hindered a safer delivery with less distress.'

Anna took many seconds to cry, and was 'floppy'. She was whisked away by a paediatrician for a short while, but was soon returned. 'I breast-fed her first at 5 p.m.,' says Sue. 'I still have the paper on which I wrote the time of every feed for the first four days. She fed well and sucked powerfully, but remained sleepy for days – she just fed and slept.' Sue and Anna went home on the fourth day, to many good wishes and gifts.

David and Sue felt their family was complete. Their children Gavin, Rosalind and Alice were thirteen, eleven and eight years old when Anna was born, and all three took great interest in her development and welfare. 'We had lovely times together,' says Sue. 'A baby could not have fitted more perfectly into an already busy manse home. She had love and cuddles galore, and Lassie the dog accepted her too, though keeping her distance.

'We had a wonderful family holiday in early August, camping on the Isle of Wight. We have a photo album just of that holiday with pictures of Anna, which we might not have taken otherwise. The weather was great and those memories of us all at our happiest are etched for ever.'

But Sue was worried about Anna. At the routine six-week check, she expressed her anxiety that Anna's head remained wobbly. The GP trainee was not unduly worried, and even Sue could see that Anna was progressing well in many ways. Although Anna appeared chubby right up to three and a half months, she put on a smaller amount of weight than the other children had done. She was gaining the required four to six ounces each week, but Sue recalled that Gavin had gained eight to eleven ounces at that stage.

When Anna had her first immunisation, Sue insisted the whooping cough jab was excluded in case of any neurological problems. Her GP, realising how concerned she had become and knowing she had been experienced over the years with the examination of hundreds of babies, made an appointment for Anna to see a paediatrician. 'I badly needed a professional paediatric opinion,' says Sue. 'Did Anna have a type of cerebral palsy? Did she have neck damage? Was it the birth?'

But Anna did develop in the way she smiled, gurgled and babbled in her cot first thing in the morning. 'What lovely, happy sounds,' recalls Sue. Anna grasped a rusk and rattle, transferring to her other hand by four months of age. She rolled over on to her back. She recognised her family.

A fortnight after her first injection, Anna had gained no more weight. Sue decided to give her some solids for the first time. But Anna took little of the baby rice, and totally rejected the bottle of milk Sue offered her. She appeared to be well satisfied with Sue's breast-milk, and seemed to take plenty. Nevertheless, Sue remained worried, and wondered if she was inadequately fed. But in time, Anna's weight began to go up again, and Sue felt much happier.

On Saturday 17 October, Anna spent much of her time out in the garden with Sue, who was clearing some of the old summer growth and the mess which had resulted from the great hurricane which had hit the south of England two days previously.

The next day was Sue's forty-first birthday. It had been a happy morning – the house had been full of the noise and bustle of birthday wishes, a cup of tea in bed, singing and opening parcels. Then David went ahead to church with the three older children, while Sue stayed at home to feed Anna.

As soon as Anna was settled in her pram – she slept mostly on her stomach, as the others had done – Sue followed, walking swiftly so she would reach the church for ten thirty. She left Anna in the crèche, with instructions on what to do if she woke. Then she went into church, where she was to lead the adult teaching session in the all-age worship service.

'There was a joyful, hopeful start to this Sunday,' says Sue. 'The week of the hurricane and devastation was over, I had reached the age of forty-one, and we were proud parents of four children. All factors seemed relevant to the subject of God's power, and the teaching of this Sunday on the story of Baal versus Jehovah.'

At about twelve o'clock, as the service was closing with song and prayer, Sue became aware of a rustling about her. Her daughter Rosalind had been called out by loud whispers. Then she realised that the crèche assistant was beckoning her, too, with the word, 'Anna'.

She rose quickly from her seat, as the crèche assistant whispered hurriedly, 'She's in the hall with Dorothy.' Sue rushed round the outside of the church to the church hall, knowing something was terribly wrong. Dorothy, Sue's close friend, had been in charge of the crèche. Now Sue found her pacing the empty church hall with Anna on her shoulder, pale and lifeless.

Sue remembers, 'I took one look and changed gear, from near panic to "in charge" and "nurse-like". While Dorothy crooned in despair and talked of how Anna had been found blue and not breathing, I tried to elicit other facts, but it was impossible to estimate how many minutes she had stopped breathing. No one was articulate.'

The memories Sue has of the next minutes are vivid, yet confused. They are memories of stepping on ground which moved unpredictably, space distorted, people sensed but unseen. Time stood still. Everything happened at once and yet also over extremes of time.

Sue ran to the church office with Anna, willing her to breathe. She laid her on the floor and gave mouth-to-mouth and heart massage.

She knows she must have shouted instructions, such as 'get the ambulance', but she can't remember doing so. Months later, she was told that she had run to the church door, holding Anna, and screamed for David to come quickly. Her cry had frozen everyone, most people still unaware until then of the drama in the church office.

She cannot tell how the scene must have appeared, but thinks church members must have been all over the place. She was aware of people coming and going, and of sobbing all around her. She knew David and the children were there, all witnessing the desperate scene, urging her on to revive Anna. She remembers David praying for them all.

For David, the scene is vivid, for ever imprinted in his memory. 'My children, Gavin, Rosalind and Alice, were on their knees with me on the floor of my church office, tears pouring from their eyes, their faces flushed as they repeated, "Anna, don't die, Anna, don't die." Sue was in front of us, Anna laid on the floor, Sue breathing into her.'

Sue continued to try to resuscitate Anna until the ambulance arrived, and she accompanied her to Casualty. And there, Sue says, 'Our beautiful youngest child, Anna Ceridwen, was pronounced dead.'

It was the week before the appointment to see the paediatrician.

The family was left alone, with Anna, in the large, white-walled clinic room. 'We wept, but somehow everything was restrained,' says Sue. 'Yet the mind's ability to plan and organise had not deserted us. I particularly knew it was vital the children had the opportunity to hold Anna and say goodbye. David, with great fortitude, stood in his black suit and clerical collar, and prayed for us all, especially Anna. We stood in a circle, clasped around in sudden grief, knowing yet unbelieving, on our own.

'I knew we could stay for ever gazing on this lifeless form of Anna, and we would have to leave quickly before some kind of dam burst. There were tears to be shed in rivers in the future, but now was not the proper time to let go. We hugged and kissed her, and David and the children left the room painfully, while I decided to place her on the brown examination couch. I turned away and left the room quickly. I told the nurse what I had done. I wanted no one to take her from us, but us to leave her in their care. I knew her soul was with God in some mystical reconstruction for eternity.'

They have little recollection of the journey home. 'But I did know that this mighty event in our small lives would bring us nearer to each other and to our God than anything else,' says Sue. 'David and I were in one unspoken mind that Christ in his Passion had come close by and somehow earth and heaven had combined right before us. Life, to death, to life.'

The last time David and Sue saw Anna was at the funeral director's, after the post-mortem. Anna was not Anna. David himself insisted on screwing down the lid of the coffin, then and there.

Anna's funeral was held in the family's home on the following Friday. About fifteen people were present, representatives from family and churches. David led it with other ministers offering prayers and readings. Psalm 139:13–18 and Mark 10:13–16 were read. David's superintendent minister attended the service in the living-room, and went on to take the committal service.

'We affirmed those precious words, "We are all one family in heaven and on earth," ' says Sue. 'That is what we believe, and what Jesus came to tell us.'

One cold November morning, the family went alone to scatter Anna's ashes. The place they had chosen was The Garth, a place where the older children had played, and where miles and miles of countryside could be seen in every direction.

'It was a time I'll never forget,' says David. 'The way we chose to reach it by car was blocked by the Water Authority digging the road up. We went round to the only other way up. It was blocked by a refuse lorry embedded in the tarmac at a sharp bend on a steep gradient.

'So we parked the car and walked about two miles uphill, the children, the dog, Sue and I, carrying the casket – in the cold, the wet and the half-light – silently, no one complaining, all set on doing what we had to do. I remember thinking as I scattered Anna's ashes and the wind blew them about at this top peak – "Those were bone fragments in the dust, of my daughter."

'The next time Sue and I went up there we did get the car up to the highest road spot,' David recalls. 'We came back to the car after being there at the top – with Anna – to find the car had been broken into, a window smashed, and Sue's bag taken, containing cards, money – and photos of Anna. Two days later a refuse-collector guy we knew found the bag in a waste-bin on a lamp-post. The money was gone but the other contents were still there.'

As a Methodist minister, David found the tragedy of losing a child was not only deeply emotional but theologically challenging. 'The morning service had included teaching on the God of Elijah,' he says. 'We had prayed to the God of Elijah for a miracle. It wasn't granted. But I wasn't angry with God. I couldn't be, and I could not be asking, "Why?" The answer was clearly, "Why not?" Others had lost their babies. I'd taken the funerals of other cot-death babies. Our family couldn't expect to be free of such loss and suffering.'

Sue adds, 'We did not so much question "Why?" as "What does it all mean?" Is 'certainty' ever reasonable when it comes to faith? Will the pain continue so intensely? How do we go on?" '

They were helped by all the prayers, cards, letters, calls, tears and meals that came in waves of love and compassion. Sue says they were stunned by such care, which came from friends far and near, Christians, those of other religions or none. When Anna was born, they had received seventy cards. When she died, more than three hundred cards and letters came flooding in. 'What a short four-and-a-half-month life can mean, to so many,' says Sue.

David and Sue say they gained strength for living not only from the care of others, but from one another, and from the children's love and chatter. And their doctor and health visitor were 'wonderful', says Sue. 'I was given time to talk, and appropriate visits. I know that professionals also feel devastated, so was grateful for their time and concern.

'The women from the mother and toddler group at church offered comfort and support – even having a collection for the Foundation for the Study of Infant Deaths – and these were quite low-income people. They wanted to discuss the spiritual and faith dimension, and I believe God used this situation to teach me and them about love in death and light in darkness.'

The superintendent minister who had taken the committal service had come back to the house after the service, and said he would visit again in a couple of days. 'He didn't,' remembers David. 'He didn't visit at all. And I found him impossible at staff meetings, insensitive, loud and useless. I never told him. But maybe I had to be angry with someone!'

Living far away from their families, Sue found it difficult to turn to them for comfort. She would often be weeping and longing to see a member of the family, but could not bring herself to phone and upset them.

The couple found great comfort from each other. 'David and I shed a lake of tears together, usually late in the evening or at moments in the day when the children were at school,' says Sue.

'I don't think either of us ever "felt" strong, or strong in faith. In fact the reverse is true. Our prayer-life made few requests. Prayer was often silence, tears and depth. Sometimes it was depressing. However, God is utterly dependable and we made trust a matter of will, not feeling. I was often surprised by strength given to me at the bleakest of moments.'

David says a regular comfort in the early weeks after Anna's death was gathering together with the family around an open coal fire. But for a busy minister, who was also involved in much ecumenical work, such moments were few and far between. David had to go straight back into work – which included officiating at funerals and babies' baptisms.

Sue felt that although individual minister friends were wonderfully supportive (especially one, bereaved of a wife and eighteen-month-old daughter in a road crash) the Church as an institution had no mechanism to remove responsibility from him, so he could have time on his own with Sue. By January 1988, he had reached a state of real exhaustion. At that point they were offered a weekend break at a cottage belonging to a Methodist who wanted it to be available to ministers in need of a holiday or retreat. They unwound and were greatly helped by the countryside, the sound of the river at the bottom of the garden, the quaint cottage and its interesting books. 'Most of all,' says Sue, 'we talked together, prayed together, and became close enough to know that our marriage would be safe, as long as we remained ourselves and trusted to the promise of Jesus – peace.

'Sex between us was again opportunity for shared contact,' she says. 'To be ultimately close, shed tears in privacy, and find a release from tension. It became "new", with added meaning. We took time to make the decision about one hundred per cent protection from pregnancy, and David was sterilised. It was a decision not made lightly, and when it was carried out, counselling was miserably lacking. We did suffer, knowing no other baby could be born. People may think us very selfish – we were in our forties, with a lovely family of three healthy live children, but we did feel a lot of pain as our four were the final family. Now we know it was right.'

During the first year after Anna's death, Sue says her feelings were at times so distressing that she felt she would die. 'I would not have cared if I had just lapsed into death and met the peace of God,' she says.

Her need to hold Anna was at a peak about seven months after she died, around the time of her first birthday. 'I wandered around the house on my own, whimpering, weeping and wailing, clutching a stuffed elephant we had made for Anna,' says Sue. 'I would have appeared demented to an outsider. I believed I could let go of my feelings as long as no one else was around. It was a private experience because there was such overwhelming emotion, although tears frequently came in public worship, with friends, watching TV, or in a shop seeing a baby.'

A few weeks after Anna's death, when Sue was in the shopping centre, she felt a strong urge to snatch a baby from a pram. 'Of course, I didn't – but I could have done,' she says. 'I kept looking in prams, a search for Anna which went on for some months, even though I knew in my rational mind she was dead and cremated.

'Denial was very strong in me,' she continues. 'I have always been quite laid back and placid, but Anna dying, suddenly and with no explanation, made me panic at times in the first months. If the children hurt themselves, or were late home or had to go to Casualty for stitches, I could not believe the way my knees shook. I would expect the worst. Even now, years later, I can over-react when it comes to the children's welfare. However, I know why I do it, so am more in charge of myself now. It has been a road to self-knowledge.'

The signs of grief displayed by the three children were, Sue says, heart-rending. But she goes on, 'Their faith showed new shades of colour and meaning. Total honesty was essential and they were denied nothing in the way of information. Emotional outpourings and anger were expected and respected. Strangely, no one was overpowered by anger – just great sadness.

'The children tell me, now, that they have their own story to tell, from their own point of view. As time goes on, David and I will learn more of how they were affected. Rosalind recently said how angry she had felt inside, although now she rejoices in the life Anna did have with us all.'

Sue prayed to be alive to the children's needs, and was 'given the gift of sleep, mainly dreamless sleep, for the first year. Only about five times did I wake after dreaming of Anna, sleeping, face hidden, in her cot. I think that I worked through her death, analysing, talking to those who would listen, writing, reading and doing so much gardening and cooking that I was exhausted by bedtime.

'I was breast-feeding, so poured milk for weeks afterwards. Even a course of medication intended to dry up the milk did not stem the supply. I believe the breast-feeding aided my grief by becoming the measure of Anna's existence in my mind. It was of interest to me that I continued to produce milk right up until eighteen months after her death. It seemed symbolic of the time it took to accept her "going". The milk clouding the water when I took a hot bath was a reminder of the reality of her life even when I had tried to put it to the back of my mind for a few hours.'

On 18 October 1988, the first anniversary of Anna's death, at the church where she had died, David's book *Sliced Bread* was launched.

'David had been working on St Luke's gospel and other books of the New Testament over several years,' says Sue. 'He wanted to produce a book dedicated to Anna, who died on St Luke's Day at 144 days, and to myself, who was born on St Luke's Day.'

The book was launched in a large company, including David's parents, his sister and her husband, and Sue's sister. 'It did help cushion the first anniversary of Anna's death,' Sue recalls. 'But I remember that November was a terrible month for me. Grieving had been put off with all the highs of a book publication.'

In August 1990, David, Sue and the children moved to the west of Scotland. Again, it was a difficult time, leaving friends and colleagues, and settling into a new area. They were on Family Credit for six months until Sue found work.

In 1991, Sue helped to set up the Cot Death Support Group in her area, and also became a 'befriender' for the Scottish Cot Death Trust. 'Happily, the death rate for Sudden Infant Death Syndrome has fallen in the last three years,' she says. 'But people in the west of Scotland are still bereaved by SIDS. All the education in non-smoking, sleep position, breast-feeding and not overheating is given by midwives, doctors and health visitors, but still babies die.'

She loves her work as a health visitor in a deprived area, with lots of new housing and community development initiatives being set up. Many of the families she visits are among the high risk groups for cot death, but in two years not one baby has died of SIDS in her practice.

'In retrospect I'm so glad that Anna existed and lived, though for a short time,' says Sue. 'Perhaps her birth "replaced" the previous pregnancy, the baby I miscarried. But I have no doubt that God has those two babies in his love – the one we knew and the one we didn't know.

'Looking back, I am thankful that the experience can continue to offer me a source of compassion for others and an awe at the fragility yet wonder of creation.

'Through the whole experience of loss, which still goes on, God came and comes near enough to be tangible. All of Jesus' life and death came to life for us. The gospel stories, the Christmas message, Good Friday and the resurrection – they all offer such hope and comfort.

'The day Anna died, David was leading a Bible-study series, and the subject that day was "Faith in God alone". How we have learnt the importance of that lesson.'

3

Ben Tyne, our little *Kai Viti*

In the middle of 1990, an advertisement appeared in the *Guardian* newspaper for a lecturer in educational psychology at the University of the South Pacific in Fiji. Liz applied for the post. She had almost given up hope of a reply when a telegram arrived at her home in Newcastle-upon-Tyne. She was offered the post on the basis of her application, without even having an interview, and was told to reply within one week.

Liz and her husband Andy had already decided they wanted to live and work in another country, so an offer like this seemed perfect. Yet their plan to live abroad had been to stay for only one year, then come back to England and start a family. The university was offering a three-year contract.

But they decided it was an offer they couldn't turn down, and Liz began work in Fiji in January 1991. Andy had no work to start with, but a few months into Liz's contract he was offered a job as a lawyer with the Fiji Government, working in the Attorney General's Chambers. His contract ran for two and a half years – so his job would finish at the same time as Liz's.

They found a flat in the middle floor of a house situated in the residential streets near the university. Several colleagues lived near by, and Andy and Liz delighted in getting used to a totally different culture. They soon made friends.

Andy and Liz found that while the Indo-Fijians were mostly Hindu, many other Fijians were Christian. But they favoured a Quaker-like approach to their faith, and together with some lecturers from a theological college, they decided to set up their own housegroup.

They enjoyed their new way of life, but at the back of their minds was the question – should we try for a baby while we're in Fiji? They had envisaged one year abroad, not three, and they both wanted a child. But could they have a baby and continue to work?

It was relatively easy to find good nannies. And when they kept coming across working mothers in Fiji who were coping well – who weren't waiting until they returned to their home country to start a family – they began to think, 'If they can do it, so can we.'

At the end of October 1991, Liz felt sure she was pregnant. Andy was going to a United Nations lawyers' meeting in Geneva, and was due to spend a weekend with family and friends in Britain. He wanted to wait until he came back to Fiji before Liz did a pregnancy test. However, Liz wanted to do the test before he left – partly because she just couldn't wait, and partly because she wanted Andy to tell the family the good news while he was in Britain.

They took the test – and it was positive.

For the first three months, Liz felt sick, and was unable to eat most of the food on offer in Fiji. But they flew to Australia to spend Christmas with Liz's cousin, and arriving late at night, very hungry, they found McDonald's open. Liz, a vegetarian, became desperate for a hamburger. She wolfed it down, stopped being a vegetarian on the spot, and food stopped being so much of a problem.

The pregnancy continued normally, and Liz felt well. The couple were looking forward to Saturday 4 July 1992, the date the baby was due. But the date came – and the baby didn't.

Liz's next ante-natal appointment was the following Tuesday, 7 July. In the early hours of that morning, when Liz was enduring her usual period of sleeplessness, she felt something in her womb. There was a rush of movement – and then stillness.

'I tried pushing the side of my tummy to get the baby to move, but there was nothing,' says Liz. 'I knew people said babies move less just before they're born, so I didn't worry too much. But looking back, it was as if the baby was struggling.'

Andy and Liz arrived at Dr Neil Sharma's surgery in time for their ten o'clock appointment. The doctor listened for the baby's heartbeat, but heard nothing. He changed the battery in his machine, and listened again. Still no heartbeat. Hoping the machine was wrong, he sent Andy and Liz to the hospital for a scan and a foetal heart monitor, saying it was 'to reassure you'. No one wanted to state what might be happening. Dr Sharma said he would join them at the hospital later.

They found a huge queue of pregnant women waiting for scans. Unable to sit and wait, Liz pushed her way forward, saying, 'My doctor couldn't find the baby's heartbeat – I need to be seen now!'

Liz and Andy watched the screen which showed their baby. There was no movement. Nobody said anything. Liz was moved to the foetal heart monitor. There was no baby pulse. Liz kept crying. Still nobody said anything.

Eventually, Dr Sharma arrived. He took them to a quiet room and said, 'We have a tragedy.' Liz remembers saying, 'You mean our baby's dead.'

Her immediate reaction was anger. 'I was two centimetres dilated at the time – so near to the baby's birth,' she says. 'I felt cheated out of our living baby.' Then practical things overtook feelings – 'I just wanted to know how we were going to get this baby out!' she says.

Dr Sharma asked Andy and Liz to decide whether they wanted the baby to be induced that day, or whether they should go home and return to the hospital the next day. Liz felt quite clear that returning the next day was unacceptable. She could not spend the night with a dead baby.

On the other hand, they wanted some time. Time to think, time to adapt, before rushing straight into a labour ward there and then. So they arranged to go home for a few hours and return to the hospital that afternoon.

Back at the flat, feelings became confused. Liz had a report to write for college – she thought she ought to write it before returning to hospital for the labour. Then she realised how absurd that was, and it came to her that she was trying to block out what was really happening. Her professor phoned; Liz told him what had happened, and found him 'incredibly supportive'. Andy was in shock, felt faint, and had to lie down for a while. Liz made herself cheese on toast. 'It was survival instinct,' she says. 'I realised that I needed sustenance for labour.'

They phoned two close friends in Fiji. One of them was out, but they left a message with others, asking her to come to the hospital later. Then they phoned their families and a close friend in England. It was one o'clock in the morning British time, so when their parents became aware of the phone ringing in the night, they thought immediately that it was the good news of the baby's safe arrival.

Andy cried as he spoke to his father, who was clearly terribly upset. It was his second grandchild to die in this way. Andy has only one sister, whose first baby was stillborn.

At the hospital that afternoon, Liz was given a pessary to start the labour. A couple of close friends arrived. 'It was a great help to have them there, supporting us,' says Liz.

At seven o'clock she was given another pessary, but still nothing was happening. Liz and Andy decided to go home after all, even though they knew the labour would begin during the night.

Liz became very practical again. 'I thought, "My body's going to go through hell, I need some sustenance." ' One friend arrived to stay the night, and two others came with a takeaway pizza. Then Liz watched *LA Law* on television – a programme she will always associate with that night.

Mild contractions started at nine o'clock, and were much stronger two hours later. Soon after midnight Andy and Liz returned to hospital with Ros, who had agreed to be with them throughout the labour, even though she was still breast-feeding her own one-month-old baby.

'We needed someone there because we were scared and away from home,' says Liz. 'I didn't know what the labour would feel like, or how my body would behave. We needed someone to be involved who would support us in a practical way, and who had been through labour herself.'

Liz was also helped by an earlier phone call from Andy's dad. He told her that a group of people from his church were meeting to pray constantly throughout the labour. During the contractions, she was able to focus on the fact that they were praying, and found it helped her through the pain.

Liz and Andy had planned an active birth, but in the circumstances

Liz chose to have painkillers 'just to get through it'. 'It was no longer an opportunity to embrace a creative labour,' she says. 'But somehow I had to face the labour, face each contraction, in order to endure it. Any medical intervention would be considered.' She chose pethidine, which dulled the pain.

She was very tired – she'd been emotionally exhausted before the labour even started – so a saline drip gave her energy. Andy massaged her throughout, which she says made a great difference to her pain. She remembers being amazingly relaxed as she lay on her side and breathed through each contraction. In the brief seconds between contractions they talked about all kinds of unrelated things, such as a trip to Amsterdam.

Much later, people in the UK seemed to be horrified that Liz had not been offered a Caesarean. But she hadn't been offered one because medically it was not seen to be the best option. Even if she had been, Liz would not have chosen a Caesarean. She felt that she had a better chance of surviving the experience psychologically if she actually delivered her baby herself, consciously experienced the delivery and met the baby. She would have accepted an epidural, but the medical facilities in Fiji at the time meant epidurals were rarely performed.

'It was very painful and traumatic, but I felt the labour was one of the few things I could positively say I had done,' says Liz. 'My body had let me down because my baby had died, but at least I could say my body worked – I'd got the baby out myself.

'Ros helped by saying I'd done well. I focused on the labour, and during it I didn't feel angry. I wasn't crying. I felt angry before and I felt angry afterwards. But during the labour I felt I just had to deliver that baby, and I concentrated on that.'

They had already chosen both a girl's and a boy's name. So when at 8.28 a.m. their baby boy was born, Liz was able to say, clearly and positively, 'It's Ben.' And she added, 'What a beautiful nose.'

'Andy cried,' Liz recalls. 'It was a cry of anguish. And he put his head on my shoulder.'

Because Andy's sister had been through the same experience, he and Liz already knew how important it was to spend time with their baby. The doctor was very sensitive, and left them alone for three-quarters of an hour.

'It was an incredibly powerful time,' says Andy. 'I held Ben, cried over him, talked to him, kissed him, sang to him. I was so aware of the fact it was to be the only time I was ever going to hold him and talk to him. It was awful, but it was also very special.

'He was still warm. I felt very strongly that he was there with us. We'd had a relationship with him while Liz was pregnant. We'd see his arm moving across her stomach. We didn't have a TV, and we'd joke that we didn't need one, we could just watch her stomach.

'I was filled with the wonder of it, this perfect little baby. I was desperately aware he wasn't alive, but I had a real feeling of him being a person, and I wanted to tell him how special he was, how much I loved him.'

Andy and Ros took photographs of Ben, and of Ben with one or both of his parents. Liz regrets now that all the photographs show a naked baby. After he had been washed, Ben was brought back to them wrapped in a white sheet – but Liz had undressed him. 'I wanted to see all of him, unwrapped,' she says. 'Really I wanted to see him alive, and I was searching for his life.'

Liz had packed clothes for him in the suitcase she had prepared for hospital. But before she was admitted for the labour she had bitterly thrown his clothes away.

Much later, she regretted not having dressed him, and not having a photo of him dressed properly. She tries to forgive herself: 'You can't think of everything you need to do when you're under so much stress, still exhausted from labour and drugged by pethidine. It was amazing we were even capable of doing what we did. It's hard, since there was only that one opportunity to do things which could have repercussions for the rest of our lives.'

Three months later, she wrote a poem about some of her feelings on greeting Ben at his birth:

I Want to See Him Alive

I let them wash him
Wanting at least to see him at his best
No fear at what I will see
Just a need
That is my baby in the nurse's arms
Why wrapped in a sheet
I want him unwrapped

I want to see all
I have so little
I look over all his perfect body
Looking for life

Later, the photos return
I look in vain for the one I want
The one of him looking like a normal baby
Why did we not dress him at birth
The one in the coffin showing all of him, not just his face
The one of him alive.

Eventually Dr Sharma returned, to take Ben for his post-mortem. Andy took a cutting of his hair, then said to Liz, 'Are you ready to say goodbye now?'

Liz recalls her feelings. 'How could I possibly have said goodbye? I hadn't even said hello. I knew I couldn't keep him, he would decompose, but I couldn't say goodbye.

'So I didn't say goodbye. I'd held him, but I hadn't kissed him. I felt awful about it afterwards, so I kissed him two days later when he was cold in the mortuary. This was much worse, but I had to do it.'

Dr Sharma had asked Andy and Liz whether they would like to have a post-mortem, even though he was sure of the cause of Ben's death. The cord had been wrapped four times tightly round his leg, and it was obstructed so much that nothing could get through from mother to baby.

Liz and Andy both wanted to be absolutely sure that nothing else was wrong, and said they would like the post-mortem. But it showed what Dr Sharma expected. Ben had been a healthy baby who probably had died of oxygen deficiency.

And because Andy's sister had lost her baby in the same way, they also wanted to be sure there was no problem in Andy's family which could have caused this double tragedy. Dr Sharma told them there could be no genetic cause, but complied with their request that blood tests should be taken to check this. Again, he was right.

Liz was taken to the maternity ward, and although she was first put in a room with a new mother and baby, they soon left, leaving her with her own room. Liz was still so tired and drained that she doesn't even remember there being a baby there.

'I was lying in the hospital bed, and Ben was in the mortuary, but I didn't really think about where he was,' says Liz. 'It didn't occur to me that I had the right to see him again, until I read later about what other parents of stillborn children have been able to do.'

Liz began to question all the things she had done which could have killed Ben. Had she done too much? Had she put him at risk by going to a Tahitian midwife? But the most traumatic question was, 'Did he die because I didn't love him enough?' This was immediately answered by Andy, who reassured her about how much she had loved her baby. 'But I had to state that fear at the beginning, to let the spectre come out and be dealt with,' says Liz. 'And I'm still dealing with it.'

Two couples from the house church, Jovili and Lisa, Jack and Lydia, arrived at the hospital to offer their support. They gathered around Liz's bed, talking, listening and praying.

'Suddenly the question of a funeral came up,' says Liz. 'I hadn't really thought about it before.'

In Fiji, there are no funeral directors. Funerals are organised by the family. Andy and Liz were suddenly very much aware that they had no family. Neither were they part of a traditional church. Yet they wanted a service and they wanted someone close to them to take it.

Fortunately, the two couples from the housegroup were also aware of these facts. Jovili felt he wanted to be their family, and took on the funeral arrangements. They asked Lydia to take the service.

One of the lowest points for Andy came when he arrived at the hospital on Thursday to take Liz home. It was unimaginable to him that they should be leaving a maternity hospital without a baby. It wasn't right.

It hit him hard. It was one of those occasions they had imagined, the three of them leaving hospital. There were many more occasions like that to come. Liz had imagined her baby's clothes hanging out on the washing-line. One of the hardest things for her was walking past a line of baby clothes. She thought, 'Why have they got a baby and we haven't; why did our baby die?'

The funeral was arranged for the next day, Friday. As there was no funeral director to collect Ben from the hospital mortuary, and his body had not been prepared, Andy and Liz decided to collect him themselves. Although the prospect was daunting at first, in the end Liz found it had a positive side.

'At least it meant we were in control,' she says. 'Nobody took it over. We had the freedom to do what we wanted with the funeral because we were in a different culture. I had a sense of peace about it. Since we were not able to look after him alive, the actions around his death became so precious.'

Some friends, Phil and Bob, had turned up with a car on the morning of the funeral. 'They hadn't said, "Let us know if you need anything," but they'd just done what needed to be done,' says Andy. 'They brought food for us, and told us they were taking us to the funeral. It was just what we needed.'

Liz had brought clothes to the mortuary, and had planned to dress Ben herself. But she found she couldn't do it, so a Fijian mortuary attendant very gently dressed him while Andy and Liz watched.

Jovili and Lisa arrived with a tiny coffin, a woven mat and a piece of traditionally printed tapa cloth. It was a Fijian custom, which has been taken over by the Christian Church, to wrap the coffin in a woven mat. A piece of tapa-bark cloth, a white cloth printed with a light brown pattern, is placed on top of the grave. It was very important to Liz and Andy that the Fijian customs were followed.

'Ben was very much our little *Kai Viti*,' says Liz. *Kai Viti*, meaning 'Of Fiji', were the words they eventually chose to write on his gravestone. 'Ben Tyne, our little *Kai Viti*. Died 7th July 1992. Born 8th July 1992.'

The mortuary attendant laid Ben in his coffin, and the two cars left for the cemetery.

'Things happened at the funeral that were so right, although it was so wrong,' says Liz.

'Death is taken very seriously in Fiji, and everyone goes to everyone's funeral. We would have been swamped, and we didn't feel we could cope with hordes of people. We only wanted close friends, so we invited about twenty people who we wanted to be there. We told everyone else, people at the university and Andy's office, that it was a private funeral. Some of them found it hard to take, but we decided we couldn't deal with other people's needs.'

The couple had carefully chosen what they wanted to place in Ben's coffin, and this they did at the cemetery. Underneath him, Liz laid a quilted cushion which she had made for him. They each wrote to Ben on the back of a postcard of Holy Island, Northumberland – a special place for them – and placed it next to him. Andy put in a soft toy platypus he had bought for the baby in Sydney, as well as bougainvillaea flowers and a photograph of Ros's daughter, who would have been his friend.

Liz felt she wanted to shout for that time never to stop, but knew that could not happen. And she felt self-conscious, wondering if all the people watching them were getting bored, and feeling that they should press on.

Ben's coffin was left open for the service. 'That wasn't something we'd planned – it just seemed to happen,' says Liz. Andy and Liz realised they wanted the friends they had invited to see him, to be witnesses to the fact that he was really there. They needed him to be acknowledged, to be talked about afterwards. People said things, like 'He's a beautiful baby,' that they needed to hear and will always remember.

'Losing a child like this is so immeasurably hard,' says Liz. 'When you've never known the child, it's hard to grieve. I had never known Ben alive, never seen him move, cry, feed, outside me.

There are no experiences, expressions, conversations, to remember. It can be hard at times to realise that the child existed at all – and yet realising his existence is so necessary to grieving. So anything that made Ben more real, such as these people seeing him, was so helpful to us in affirming his existence. We recorded the service, and that was a further affirmation. People in Britain could hear the tape and grieve with us.'

After the funeral, Liz knew she needed time and space to mourn. She knew there was no point rushing back to work in an attempt to block out what had happened. She chose to take her full twelve weeks' maternity leave, taking the time that she would have been with Ben in his early weeks, and using it to grieve for him.

'I felt the loss of the days ahead,' she says. 'Days which were to be filled with looking after my child stretched emptily ahead.'

She spent several days, in the weeks following Ben's death, learning Fijian mat-weaving from a wonderful Fijian woman called Makereta Sotutu. Makereta, being very old and near to death herself, didn't fear death, and was able to offer Liz much support. Liz found the weaving absorbing and therapeutic.

'I knew there were things I had to do to get through this,' she says. 'Looking back, I realise I was clear in sorting out what I needed to do to grieve, and in going for it, whatever people thought of me. Pain is to be faced. Ben, our child, dying, giving birth to him, burying him, was the most serious, awful thing that had ever happened to me. I had to face it all. If I didn't, I felt it would create serious problems.'

Andy agrees. 'It happened to us, and it needed a response,' he says. 'People become emotional time-bombs if they don't respond to their feelings and deal with them. I was self-centred about it. I felt I needed to do things, starting with wanting to be with Ben and hold him after he was born, and then having a proper burial.

'We're quite strong as individuals, and we're quite strong as a couple,' he continues. 'It's helped us. At various times in our lives we've had to face up to things and deal with them. It's a question of making choices and getting what you want out of life.'

They were each able to help the other. 'I know it drives some people apart, and I didn't know how it would affect us,' says Liz, 'but most of the time we were similar in the way we grieved and the way we wanted to express it. I would often find the mornings the worst, and might wake up crying, or with a waking dream of not being able to cry and feeling I was suffocating. Andy seemed to be saddest at night. Yet despite this, and because we talked about it, we grew closer and closer. Andy was the only person who really understood my feelings, and who really felt Ben's death as I did, since we were both his parents. And I found him so supportive, being with me and allowing me to cry, and talking about feelings.'

Liz found she really needed letters and calls from friends and family in England to support her. 'I told one friend that if people at home were feeling desperate to help, just tell them to ring me and let me cry on the phone. I needed to be allowed to express my feelings. I had two or three calls a day after that. I couldn't have coped without them. It made me feel less lonely, and in talking I realised my own feelings.'

Letters from the UK had the same effect, and Liz often cried as she read them. Sometimes she had to leave them for a while. They spoke of the awfulness of what had happened, and of how Andy and Liz would have been good parents. 'Who knows?' says Liz. 'But I needed to hear that.'

Some people sent helpful books. One poetry book was so moving that Andy found he had to limit himself to one poem a day, and cried after reading each one.

'All our friends were great,' says Liz. 'That's something positive that's come out of it – the incredible love and care of friends. I've kept my confidence in people.'

A group of friends in Newcastle phoned Liz and Andy, saying they were planning to hold a memorial time for Ben. They contacted anyone who knew the couple, and invited them to attend.

About twenty adults with lots of children gathered at Druridge Bay, a large sandy beach on the Northumberland coast which was a favourite place of Liz and Andy. It was windy, as was usual there, but also sunny. The group sat in a circle, and in the centre was a bowl, a jar of water from the Tyne river, photos of Liz and Andy with Ben, and letters written to Ben from his parents. A few people read out the poems that Liz and Andy had included in Ben's funeral. One friend, Helen, who had had a baby two weeks before Ben, read a poem written by parents surviving the death of their child.

Earlier, other friends, Jane and Richard, had gone to a beautiful place where the North and South Tyne meet and collected some water in a jar. This was a special place for Ben, since he was given the name Tyne after the river. In the memorial time at Druridge Bay, the water was emptied into a bowl, and the bowl was taken to the sea and the water poured away – a Celtic ritual representing the soul of the dead person being carried down the river to the sea.

'They were remembering Ben, and then releasing him,' says Liz. 'They were so helpful. It helped so much, it was marvellous.'

Liz's parents came to Fiji for two weeks. Her father was unwell, and having to look after someone else actually helped Liz. 'Their presence surprised me by giving me a feeling of healing,' she says. 'I was able to focus on them some of the caring energy I had wanted to give to Ben. We could show them Fiji, and in doing so remember the Fiji we loved.'

Her father found it hard to express his feelings, but his determination to make the trip to Fiji, against doctor's orders, and his need to visit Ben's grave, showed Liz how deeply he felt Ben's death. Her mother had lost a child, Liz's elder sister, when baby Anne was three months old. It helped Liz to find in her mother someone who was willing and able to recognise her pain.

Both she and Andy felt a great need to grieve with family and friends, and at the beginning of September they returned to England for six weeks. Being with close friends who could cry with them was very important. It was hard, however, for Liz to visit her sister Becky, who had a new healthy baby girl. But Liz and Andy, and Becky and Richard, felt they should meet and try to face the problem head on.

When they returned to Fiji and visited the graveyard, they found that they were at first unable to identify where Ben was buried. For several frightening minutes, Liz even feared someone had moved him. They knew things grew very fast in Fiji, but they had never grasped quite how fast. They had only been away for six weeks. 'Ben had died, a major, awful loss. But to lose his grave would be almost like a further death,' says Liz.

In contrast to all the things which helped, Liz found many things in the early days which didn't help at all. Chief among these were acquaintances who didn't want to talk about what had happened, or who wanted Andy and Liz to meet *their* needs to help.

'Basically they were uncomfortable with the level of our grief and they wanted us to move on,' says Liz. 'Their attitude was, "You're young, you're healthy, so you can get on and have another child." It was totally insensitive. They were not recognising our child. Someone actually said, "This has really affected you, hasn't it?", as if they were surprised.'

Liz felt very angry with people who found it difficult or embarrassing to talk about what had happened. She never expressed her anger, but she felt, 'You may think this is hard for you, but it's worse for me.'

Andy found the world divided into two – there were those who were sympathetic and understood the fact that the couple must be mourning deeply, and who could face up to the fact that they'd lost Ben. And there were those who couldn't.

'It was as though our acquaintances had divided into two groups, sheep and goats,' he explains.

One acquaintance, a woman in charge of local campaigns for breast-feeding, said, four days after the birth, 'You've got to look ahead now.' Earlier, on the day of the birth itself, she had said, 'I know how you feel – I'm having difficulty conceiving my fourth child'!

A couple of weeks later, when that same woman phoned to ask Liz if she could visit her, Liz was still so angry that she refused her visit, and explained why. She told her she was surprised that someone who spent so much time around new and expectant mothers could be so insensitive. The woman apologised.

Generally, they felt that if a person's response was genuine, if they spoke from the bottom of their heart, however clumsily, then whatever they said was right. But if someone had to think hard about the 'proper' thing to say, it was sometimes wrong. A friend's child sent them a card which said, 'I hope your next one will be a success.' From an adult, it would have been insulting, with its inference that Ben had been 'unsuccessful'. But from a child, who wrote it in sympathy and love, it was helpful.

Another friend's child asked, ten months later, if Ben had died because of something Liz had done. 'From an adult, this would have been horrific,' says Liz. 'But because it came from a child, I valued Joe's honesty and openness, and welcomed the opportunity to explain about the cord.'

They didn't necessarily find it good to talk to people who had had a similar experience. It helped, although it was sad, to feel they were not the only ones, and to know someone else had been through it – and there was always a bond with people who had been through it. But often the most helpful people were those who allowed Liz and Andy to express whatever it was they were feeling.

The housegroup in Fiji was changing, and one Sunday a couple came with a baby a few weeks older than Ben would have been. Baby David even had the same colour hair. Feeling very upset at seeing the baby, Andy and Liz had to leave for a while, although they returned later. Afterwards, they felt angry that they hadn't been warned.

'Yet in the end it helped me to face up to things,' says Liz. 'I faced the fact that David had a right to live. It helped me to grieve when he reached a milestone that Ben would have reached. When David started walking, I was able to grieve that our baby didn't walk.'

David's mother, Carrie, and Liz eventually became friends. But it took a time of crisis for Liz to be able to phone Carrie and cry, and the block of David was always there.

Liz says all the anger she felt was not directed at God. 'I don't think God is responsible for what happened. I don't feel that it's part of God's plan when someone dies, a baby who hasn't lived. Ben didn't have his life and there's no way that's right.

'It's wrong. That's my ending point – it's just wrong. I have tried very hard to make something creative out of what happened – to rebuild my life in a creative way, integrating the pain of having Ben – but that doesn't make it right.'

Andy, meanwhile, was searching to make sense of things. 'I identified with Job,' he says. 'Three months after Ben died, Liz's dad died. Then nine months after that, my mum died. I keep asking, "Where is God in all this?" And there's no answer. But something else is saying to me, "Yes, God is there." I do believe God's somewhere, but I don't have the answers.

'Faith is a journey, and it involves discovery and pain,' he continues. 'We should pursue it. I felt like the travellers in *Pilgrim's Progress*, and this is the deepest and most painful experience I've ever had. It doesn't take away my faith, or strengthen my faith, but it's part *of* my faith.

'The picture of the crucified Jesus, and the pain that must be suffered when your son dies, is helpful. To see God as a suffering father, knowing how much it must have hurt him, is a helpful image to me. But I can't simply look at that and feel better.'

Andy and Liz felt almost immediately after Ben died that it was important to both of them to have another baby soon. It was also important that they should try to have the baby before they left Fiji.

Seven months after Ben died, Liz became pregnant again.

She describes her second pregnancy as an emotional hell. Sometimes, if the baby didn't move, she was convinced it was dead. But when it was moving rapidly, she feared it was in difficulty – the cord must be wrapped round.

She bought herself a hand-held heart monitor, so that whenever she was worried she could listen to the baby's heartbeat. Once or twice, when she was at work, she couldn't feel the baby moving, and she rushed back to the flat in a panic, attached the monitor – and was reassured by hearing the regular heartbeat.

Because of Liz's fear that Ben had died because she didn't love him enough, she and Andy kept talking to this baby. They wanted to let it know it was wanted. 'We do want you to come out and play with us,' they would say. But Liz couldn't prepare a quilted cushion for the baby, as she had for Ben. And they found it hard to buy anything for the baby before the birth.

'But the question, "Is this baby going to live?" still wouldn't be answered until the birth,' says Liz. 'So I buried myself in work. I was so relieved I had an interesting, involving job.

'I felt angry as well. Why did I have to go through two pregnancies and two labours to have just one child?' But however angry and bad-tempered she became, she says Andy remained 'incredibly supportive'.

Liz was very big and uncomfortable, and she had the constant feeling that only when the baby was born could some important aspects of her life continue. Two weeks before the baby was due, Liz asked to be induced. She felt she just had to know the baby was safe. Dr Sharma was sympathetic, and arranged for her induction on Wednesday 13 October 1993.

Throughout the labour, Liz cried – but not because of the pain. 'It wasn't excruciatingly painful. I cried for Ben. I just let go and grieved for him. I sobbed and sobbed. I didn't know it was going to be like this – the tears just came. Looking back, I realised I had never really grieved the labour. I had to remain very much in control during Ben's labour in order to survive it. So it surprised me when the tears came in my second labour, but maybe I needed to feel the emotional pain of Ben's labour in order to go through the process again. It made the second labour harder, but perhaps it was the only way.'

A friend, Sarah, helped Andy to support Liz through the labour. It was longer than Dr Sharma had anticipated, and when the baby was showing signs of distress towards the end, forceps were used. And so their second son entered the world.

He opened his eyes, held his arms out to Liz and latched on to her breast straight away. The couple's relief was overwhelming. 'I just couldn't believe it,' Liz says.

Robin Mana Tyne weighed 7lb 15oz – almost exactly the same as his brother. Andy also recalls how much he looked like Ben, although Liz says she didn't notice that at the time.

'We both bonded and loved and were overwhelmed by Robin straight away,' says Liz. The morning after he was born, when Liz was in the shower, Andy arrived at the hospital. He picked Robin up from the bed – a little cocooned bundle – and was overtaken by a powerful emotion: 'This is my baby.' The emotional moment was shared by Liz when, returning from the shower, she saw Andy cuddling their child.

'Before the birth I was a little worried I wouldn't bond with Robin, or that I'd become depressed, as a reaction to Ben's death and to the extreme need to have another child,' says Liz. 'I am so relieved that neither happened – I just fell in love with Robin, and enjoy him.'

The following Sunday, they went to the housegroup at Carrie's home – to find the session had been cancelled for that day, and a party was being held for Robin instead.

And a further party was held at the home of the British Ambassador, whom the couple knew quite well. He offered his home for a lunch party, so Andy and Liz could invite their friends to celebrate the fact that Robin had safely arrived.

'It was as if the whole of Fiji was rejoicing with us when Robin was born,' says Liz.

Just as they found it important to celebrate, they also felt they had to take Robin to Ben's grave. 'It was important to recognise them as two different children,' says Liz.

'There were many things I felt I couldn't work out about Ben until I had another baby,' she says. 'Now Robin's here, I've separated my grief for "a baby" from "Ben, the baby".

'Robin makes a lot of things a lot better – we are so very grateful – but he does confuse things.

'Everything we have with Robin is what we didn't have with Ben,' Liz continues. 'I almost resent feeling the pain now, because Robin is so funny and sweet and lovely. But eventually I know I'm going to have to re-grieve Ben. But not now.'

'It's as if we've put Ben on the top shelf,' says Andy. 'We've not forgotten him, but our feelings about him are not being dealt with at the moment. The experience of Robin has blocked out the feelings about Ben.

'For a time after Robin was born, I didn't think about Ben, and that wasn't good. Feelings can get stored up. We both feel a responsibility to Robin to face up to Ben, because we don't want to dump our feelings on Robin in some way.

'It's not that we want to cling on to Ben in some morbid way, because that's not helpful either,' Andy goes on. 'But you need to sort out your feelings at different stages of the journey of life, just as you understand God in different ways on that journey. You have to re-evaluate your understanding and feelings as different things happen. So we don't want to dwell endlessly on

Ben, but we do have to make sense of Ben in the light of Robin.'

After Ben died, Andy and Liz felt they needed everyone they met to know that they had had a baby, but that he had died. Slowly, they reached the stage of not having to shout it out to the world. After Robin was born, when people asked if he was their first child, they would sometimes say yes.

They found it sometimes depended on who was asking the question. When a taxi driver asked if Robin was their first child, Andy felt he was unlikely to meet this man ever again, so didn't need to explain. So he said yes. But when someone he is likely to get to know better, and see again, asks if Robin is the first, Andy explains that he is the second.

Even so, when he says Robin is the first, he still feels guilty. 'Ben doesn't deserve that response,' he says. 'I feel as if I'm denying him.' Liz agrees: 'We are a family of four, it's just that one of us isn't here.'

'I don't want Robin to take Ben's place,' says Andy. 'I feel guilty about it. Again, we don't want to make an icon of Ben, but it is important to acknowledge him.'

At times, they have to remind themselves that all this has happened to them. 'I sometimes catch myself thinking, "Did I really have that child?"' says Liz. 'I find it hard to grasp that I really did have another baby.'

But in the same way, they also find it difficult to believe in the existence of Robin. Months after the birth they still asked each other, in relief and wonder, 'Have we really got a child?'

The relief shows itself in countless ways. 'We can go into Mothercare now,' says Liz, simply. And although not many people are thrilled by washing the clothes, Andy and Liz took a photo of the first washing-line with Robin's clothes on it.

And when Robin keeps them awake in the night, Liz thinks, 'So what? I was desperate for a baby to wake me up in the night after Ben was born.'

But at the same time, she is realistic enough to allow herself to feel annoyed, especially when she feels exhausted and has a particularly bad night. And inevitably, she keeps checking Robin is still breathing.

Andy doesn't get impatient with Robin at all. 'I just value the fact that he's alive, that he's who he is,' he says. 'When you've been through a situation like this, you realise you have to take the good times and the bad times, and all are precious.'

Robin's arrival has also given Liz confidence – in herself, and in the future.

'When Ben died, it shattered my ability to plan for the future,' she says. 'Ben died in July 1992, my dad at the end of October 1992, then Andy's mum in June 1993. I was terrified something was going to happen to Andy. I wanted to be with him all the time, and really needed him.

'I also felt terribly old, ancient, the age I might possibly be if my child had died at a more normal age, when I was in my seventies, say. Robin's arrival made me feel young again. A supreme breeze of life.

'Now my trust in the future is back, because of Robin, even though I feel this trust is an illusion. I value being able to live a normal life, to say, "next week, I'll do this." The whole experience has made me appreciate and enjoy things, and be lighter about them.'

Now Robin is here, Liz is also able to acknowledge that different people can grieve and worry over different experiences. After Ben died, when she heard anyone worrying because their baby was ill, her immediate and angry response was, 'At least your baby is still alive.' Now she realises it's valid to worry about a child's health – or any other problem – even though it may not be 'as bad' as her own experience.

She would love to have another baby, going through a normal pregnancy and labour, without feeling the anxiety, fear and anger she felt when she was expecting Robin. But she also feels that to go through pregnancy and labour a third time would be another risk, potentially normalising but potentially further grief.

'I desperately need *this* child, Robin,' she says. 'We may try for another in a year or so, but that would be extra.

'We still grieve for Ben. Sometimes it hurts like before. There's still much to work through – but not with the same intensity or urgency. Maybe it will always be like this.'

4

Waiting for Lauren

When Jacqui had her first miscarriage, she didn't even know she was pregnant. She and David had been married for three and a half years when, in October 1990, they decided to consult their doctor. They were concerned that after nine months of trying Jacqui had still not become pregnant. The doctor agreed to start tests, but first took a pregnancy test to make quite sure Jacqui wasn't already pregnant, as her period was late. The result was negative.

'David did a sperm test, and the day the results came back, I had the miscarriage,' says Jacqui. 'It was ironic. The pregnancy test had been negative because my body was already in rejection.'

Jacqui had been to visit a friend that morning. While she was there, she'd looked at herself in the mirror. 'I said to my friend, "If I didn't know any better, I'd swear I was pregnant." Back at home, I was having lunch, and suddenly felt a desperate urge to go to the loo. And there it was in the toilet pan. The doctor said it was a part of a membrane, but to me it was a baby. It looked like a baby.'

But Jacqui says she recovered quickly from the shock and loss. Her main reaction was relief – she now knew she could get pregnant. 'I had the feeling, "I've had my miscarriage now, so it's over with. It'll be fine now,' she recalls.

Within a week, both Jacqui and David were back at work. David was part of a church pastoral team, and the couple were living on the premises in the top flat. Their families lived a three-hour drive in different directions. The church were no strangers to miscarriage, and neither over-reacted nor ignored the news. The church staff, in particular, were supportive.

Their GP suggested they wait three months before trying for another baby. And in January 1991, the first month they tried again, Jacqui became pregnant.

As soon as she knew she was pregnant again, Jacqui felt positive. She was healthy, and describes the next weeks as 'plain sailing'. But David was concerned. 'I'm naturally the more cautious of the two of us,' he says. 'It was Jacqui I was concerned about, not the baby. How would she react if it went wrong again?'

They waited until Jacqui was eight weeks into her pregnancy – past the time she'd lost the first baby – before they made the news public. 'Everyone was very supportive,' says Jacqui.

They decided to go ahead with a holiday abroad, which they'd already booked. While they were away, Jacqui was very sick with what she thought was food poisoning, and a few days after they returned, she started to feel concerned that something was going wrong.

'I can't explain what it was,' she says. 'I told the doctor I felt uneasy, and had a niggling feeling something was not quite right. I'd had a tiny spot of blood, and he told me to rest. He arranged a scan quickly to put my mind at ease.'

Jacqui lay on the couch with David sitting beside her while the scan was going on. 'It was obvious the radiographer couldn't find a heartbeat, although no one was saying anything,' says David. 'He kept moving the scanner round and round, but there was no hope on his face, and I knew what he was going to say. I was bracing myself.'

'I started crying then,' says Jacqui.

The eleven-week baby was perfectly formed, but it was dead. 'I found that really difficult,' says David. 'I'd worked as a porter in Casualty for four years and I'd seen some awful things, but it's different when it affects you directly.'

Jacqui and David were sent to a ward, but were told a D&C couldn't be performed immediately. They were sent home, and told to return the next day.

'That was the hardest time,' says Jacqui. 'You know the baby's dead inside you, and there's a part of you that just wants it taken away. How do you spend the time? You know there's nothing you can do to harm the baby, so there's no reason not to do anything. But you can't plan to do anything. We were in a state of limbo. We were alone in the flat, but we still had to walk the dog, and things like that.'

David says that the dog was one of the things that kept him going throughout the time of the miscarriages. 'There was always the routine task of walking the dog. It was something you had to do. It was almost as if he rose to the occasion, and they say animals can pick up tensions, sadness. He was a help.'

When Jacqui returned to hospital, she was in a room on her own, and felt the nurses didn't seem to know why she was there. 'It was all a bit strange,' she recalls. 'The sister gave me a few leaflets about miscarriage, statistics, and information about the Miscarriage Association (which I never got in touch with), but nobody said anything else. We would have welcomed someone coming to talk to us.'

'It would have been helpful,' David agrees. 'We got through it all right in the end, but then when you have to, you do. I felt let down. God created this baby, and it seemed unfair, giving with one hand and taking away with the other. What was the point of it? What could you learn from that? Retrospectively, I suppose you can talk about it with authority, which may help people. I looked back and my mind searched for reasons why this should happen. "Has God got a good reason for this?" I felt angry. Angry at God, and just plain angry. It lasted for some time.'

'It seemed cruel, allowing me to become pregnant and then taking the baby away,' says Jacqui. 'Although not so much cruel, more a waste of time. I wasn't bitter – I was bewildered. If the reason we were going through this was to help other people, then quite frankly I didn't want to help other people. You can use that reason as a cop-out. It must be for us to learn something, as individuals. But I still can't say now that I fully understand what God was trying to teach us. It's a mystery.'

Jacqui felt that their church found the second miscarriage diffi-cult to handle. 'They were all right after the first one,' she says. 'The church as a whole can accept one miscarriage, that's allowed. Once it's multiple, you get the feeling they think it's careless.' The people who helped them most were the church staff, and family and friends who visited them.

To complicate matters further, during the D&C operation Jacqui was found to have a growth. After a biopsy, she was told she had endometriosis – a condition in which tissue that lines the womb escapes to other parts of the body, and can cause cysts. Jacqui's doctor advised her to get pregnant as soon as possible, as it could be that time was short.

To get away from the situation for a while, she visited her parents, then went to France for a couple of weeks with the family.

One morning, during the stay at her parents' home, Jacqui was lying in bed feeling she must be to blame for the miscarriages; God must be punishing her for something. 'I said to God, "I'm not getting up until you tell me what I've done wrong, if anything." It was intense. And all God said was get up, carry on. When I told a friend about it later, she just laughed. But it was a profound moment. I knew there had been an encounter between me and God. It was like the account in the gospels, where Jesus says, "Take up your bed and walk." From that moment I stopped beating myself up, accusing myself, and it was laid to rest.

'I identified with Sam, Tom Hanks' character in the film *Sleepless in Seattle*, who says, "I'm going to get out of bed and breathe in and out all day long, and after a while I won't have to remind myself to get out of bed in the morning and breathe in and out." I was going to carry on. But I still didn't understand why it had all happened.'

Jacqui found the break had been helpful, and when she got home, in August, she was ready to talk about getting pregnant again. By September, she was pregnant. This time she felt 'different' – she experienced all the normal symptoms of pregnancy, and there was no sign of anything being wrong. David was still wary, but they decided to tell people the good news.

The doctor again arranged an early scan to reassure them all was well. In November, ten weeks into the pregnancy, Jacqui again climbed up on to the couch, and David stood beside her. And again, the radiographer moved the scanner round and round Jacqui's abdomen, his eyes gazing hopelessly at the screen, and they both knew that again they were going to hear the word, 'Sorry . . .'

'After about twenty seconds, I knew,' says David. 'You could see something was wrong, and there was no doubt what he was going to say. I thought "Here we go again." '

The scan found fragments of baby, but nothing perfectly formed. 'A blighted ovum,' they were told.

They were given three choices: stay in hospital for a D&C, go to talk to their GP, or go home for two weeks and then return for another scan. They weren't emotionally ready to go straight ahead with the D&C, but neither were they able to do nothing for two weeks. They chose to see their GP.

He saw them at his home, but wasn't able to offer any hope. They could wait for two weeks if they wanted to, he said, but there was no evidence to suggest the baby was alive.

'So we went to the shops and bought a dressing-gown for Jacqui,' says David. 'And then she went back into hospital the following day.'

Jacqui found it weird that she was admitted to the same ward as she had been in for the first D&C, and on duty were the same sister, the same nurse and the same man who took her down to theatre.

'Once you've had three miscarriages,' says Jacqui, 'it's a completely different ball game. We were told not to try again until we'd had tests, but we had to wait six months before the tests could begin.'

During those months, Jacqui and David were able to grieve. They grieved in different ways, and often separately, but they didn't find that it pulled them apart.

'You deal with all the medical bits,' says Jacqui, 'and then you're left with emotions and feelings, and it's difficult to talk about them. Life gets in the way. There's a lot that's been unsaid. I don't think David knows completely how I feel, and I don't know completely how David feels. But there was a general understanding. I guess we were kind on each other.

'There have been times, especially at anniversaries, when I've said to David, "I'm physically missing the babies, like a relative I've known for years – I wish they were here." I've had that feeling a lot, and I often cry at those times. He doesn't tell me it's time to put it behind me, or to stop feeling like that.'

'You can't disown your experiences of the past,' agrees David. 'At those times I'd give her a hug, or we'd talk.

'In our relationship, we try to leave space for each other to be individuals,' he goes on. 'Sometimes I want to be alone for an afternoon, and that's not a problem. It's like taking a step back from the situation, in order to try and understand it more clearly.

'I grieved in my own way. I'm a private person in emotions, but I've learned not to bottle things up. I didn't cry – not that I'm afraid to cry, but I never felt I needed to. But that's not to say I didn't feel upset. And I never got depressed. I felt low sometimes, mainly because I didn't understand why it had happened. Men find it difficult to talk to men, so I didn't talk to anyone. I suppose I dealt with my emotions on a drip-feed basis, bit by bit. I just plodded on. I'm more of a realist now than I ever was. I deal with things by putting my mind to a task, and getting on with it.'

'I didn't have a problem about David not crying,' says Jacqui. 'And whatever reaction I had, I told myself it was normal. It was okay to cry, okay not to have the words to explain it. If I had to leave church or cry in church, that was fine. One particular day, I felt a physical pain – the grief was so real, so tangible, it was awful. But I was determined not to be frightened by it, but to give myself time. The same goes for laughing – I felt the freedom to laugh.'

Even so, Jacqui feels the loss of the babies dominated her life. For David, it was different. 'I was in a very busy job in a church of six hundred, and I was out most evenings,' he says. 'Although Jacqui was doing some research, she was based at home, so had more time to think about it all.'

Jacqui doesn't remember feeling a specific emotion of anger. 'But I can think of other ways in which it was manifest,' she says. 'I can remember saying to God, "This is an absolute waste of my time" – and I guess that is anger. It was a year out of my life, which isn't long, but in terms of getting over it, it was a lot longer. When I think of those years, I was either getting pregnant, being pregnant, or getting over being pregnant.'

Sometimes, when people tried to talk to them about what happened, they'd say something insensitive or upsetting. 'How can you blame them?' asks David. 'I've tried to put myself in their shoes, and see how I'd deal with it. We all get it wrong sometimes. I'd just say to them, "You've put your big welly in it, haven't you?" '

Jacqui adds, 'We got a few comments, such as "It's nature's way" or "It was probably handicapped". They were really the wrong things to say.'

Often the pain that other people caused was unintentional. On one occasion, a friend from their homegroup had been on holiday, so although he'd known that Jacqui was pregnant, he'd not heard that she'd miscarried. When the group met one evening, he prayed for her, gave thanks for the life of the baby, and prayed for it to be kept safe. Everyone else in the group knew Jacqui had lost the baby, and kept their heads bowed. Jacqui looked up, and met the eyes of her GP, who was a member of the group. They smiled at each other. 'It was hard to tell our friend afterwards – he was devastated,' says Jacqui.

Tests began in May 1992. Both Jacqui and David were put through a whole gamut of tests, but no one could find any reason for what had happened. Every miscarriage had been different. The couple's GP suggested they ought to be in the medical books. And the doctor at the hospital told them it was 'just bad luck'.

'There was no other way he could explain it,' says David. 'He was in a cul-de-sac; there was nowhere else he could go.'

By summer 1992 they were given the medical 'all clear' to try again. But they were moving to a new area in September; David was to begin work at another church, and Jacqui was working part-time as a consultant for a Christian organisation. She felt she couldn't cope with a pregnancy at the same time. They wanted to wait until they were settled.

At Christmas, they decided the time was right. But unlike the previous occasions, Jacqui didn't become pregnant straight away.

During the months of waiting, Jacqui had to ask herself many questions. Would she ever get pregnant? What if she never had a child? What would she do if there wasn't a happy ending?

'I found that frightening,' Jacqui admits. 'I'd just assumed we'd have a family, so what was I going to do with the rest of my life? We talked about that for some time. I got more and more involved with work, and I was making mental plans of what I'd do. I wanted to deal with it. I didn't want to assume there'd be a happy ending.'

After her first miscarriage, it had helped Jacqui to see a woman in her church who had had four miscarriages, but now had three children. But now, after having three miscarriages herself, she started to be exasperated by such stories.

'People always seemed to know someone who'd had one miscarriage more than I'd had, but went on to have three children. When I'd had two miscarriages, someone knew someone else who'd had three. When I'd had three, there was someone who knew someone who'd had four. People were trying to be kind, but it used to annoy me. What I really wanted to hear was not that Auntie Joan's best friend's neighbour's sister had eight miscarriages and now has four lovely children – I wanted to hear about someone who had three miscarriages and still had no children. Because that was the question in my mind.

'I was completely unrealistic, because people weren't going to say that. But I got tired of the happy ending. I was so aware that for many people it's not like that.'

It was May 1993 before Jacqui became pregnant again.

Jacqui felt different about this pregnancy. When she knew she was pregnant, she rang her sister and found herself saying, 'I think this one is all right, and I think it's a girl.'

And even David felt different. He was optimistic; this time, he thought, everything will be all right. Even when the scan was arranged for eight weeks, he only felt slightly apprehensive – this, after all, was the third scan to be arranged early because of Jacqui's history.

The scene was the same. Jacqui was again on the couch, David was again beside her, the radiographer again searched the screen. After long seconds of waiting, Jacqui and David were told that there was no sign of a baby in the uterus.

The radiographer told them there would have to be an internal scan to confirm her findings. She suggested they sit in the waiting-room while she went to find a midwife. Jacqui, furious at being told to wait in a public place, said there was no way they would sit in the waiting-room. They were taken instead to the staffroom.

The midwife came to see them, and together they talked about what would happen next. 'We were discussing it as if it was all over,' recalls Jacqui. 'They were concerned about putting me through a third D&C because of the possible damage to the uterus, and suggested it may be better if the baby came away naturally.'

But the internal scan found the baby, safe in the womb.

They were told to go back two weeks later for a re-scan, to confirm all was well. Jacqui felt as though they were on an emotional roller-coaster. David found it difficult to accept the news.

'I didn't believe them,' he says. 'Not right away, anyway. Was the machine playing tricks? Was there really a baby? Even when I left the hospital that day, I was only seventy-five per cent of the way there. It wasn't until the third scan, at sixteen weeks, that I put most of the doubts out of my mind.'

Looking back on it, Jacqui knows this was a normal pregnancy in every way. But there was always the fear that something would go wrong. 'I looked forward to feeling the baby moving,' she says. 'But then, when it did start to move, I began to worry about how long it had been since it last moved. There was an underlying fear when the midwife or doctor listened for the heartbeat. You'd have thought I'd be desperate to hear it. But I didn't want to "wait" to hear it. Once I was over the threshold of the threat of miscarriage, I started to worry about stillbirth, or everything going wrong at the last minute.'

The couple received support from many people. At work, Jacqui's office was moved from the top to the bottom floor, so she wouldn't have all the stairs to climb.

Jacqui's due-date came and went. One evening, when she was a week overdue, she and David were leading a homegroup at their home. At about nine thirty, she started to feel uncomfortable and decided to go to bed. By the time David had finished the meeting and taken everyone home, Jacqui was having mild contractions. And by midnight, with the contractions coming every ten minutes, she decided it was time to go to hospital.

Jacqui and David arrived at the hospital at 1 a.m. The labour continued normally, with Jacqui using gas and air as the only form of painkiller. Their daughter, Lauren Joanna, was born at 6.36 a.m. on Thursday 17 February 1994. She weighed 7lb 12oz. Jacqui was able to walk back up to the ward, and left for home the following morning.

'We were both very excited,' says Jacqui. 'I felt on a high for days. It was such a special time.'

When Lauren's birth was announced in their previous church, there were cheers. And David stopped counting at two hundred and fifty congratulations cards. 'People were also able to say they were sorry for what we'd been through,' says David. 'Lauren gave them the opportunity to express themselves, which they had found difficult to do up until that point.'

Three months after Lauren was born, without warning, Jacqui had a letter from the local blood transfusion centre. A doctor wanted to visit and take a blood sample. Jacqui questioned it, and was told the antibodies in her blood were exceptionally high. What normally happens in such cases is that the baby is miscarried, yet for some reason Lauren went to full term. It could take up to a year for the antibodies to go down to a safe level, she was told, and if she became pregnant again within one year the chances of another miscarriage were high. 'That could explain the other miscarriages, but we'll never know for certain,' says Jacqui.

Jacqui considers Lauren is her fourth child. But if anyone asks if Lauren's her first, Jacqui says she is – although it pains her to say it. 'Sometimes I'll say she's my fourth pregnancy – but even that sounds like a betrayal. Society and convention dictate that you don't give explanations.'

David tells people that Lauren is their first, 'but she was a long time coming'. He sometimes gazes at her and thinks, 'You're so special, I thought you'd never be here.'

Less than a year after Lauren's birth, Jacqui had already started to ask herself: is this going to be my only one? Would we be prepared to go through it all again – three miscarriages – to have another full-term baby? She isn't sure. But David asks, 'How can we know unless we go down that path? It wouldn't put me off, but I'd consider what it would mean for Jacqui.'

Neither Jacqui nor David feel they treat Lauren any differently than they would if the miscarriages hadn't happened. They're both busy, and when Lauren wakes in the night, they don't rush to her with enthusiasm. David looks after Lauren on weekday mornings, while Jacqui works. Then she takes over, and David works for the rest of the day, and usually the evening too. 'I do get tired,' says Jacqui, 'and I'm not always pleased to see Lauren at three in the morning. I don't feel guilty about that – just normal.'

Even having been through three miscarriages, Jacqui doesn't feel better equipped to help other women in similar situations. Every person is different, she believes. 'I was aware of the emotions I might expect to go through. But when it actually happened, there was a naïvety. It's different – you can't prepare yourself for it. People ask me what they should say to a friend who has had a miscarriage, and I say, "Don't minimise it; allow them to unload their grief if they want to. But most of all, listen." '

She was often helped herself by looking at other people's situations, which seemed worse than what she was going through. 'I know it's trite to say there's always someone worse off than you,' says Jacqui. 'But it's true. I heard a woman give a testimony that amazed me. Her three children had been killed in a fire, she was disabled, her husband had died, and she was only in her forties. She said she could still stand there and say God is good and life is good.'

Jacqui chose to look positively on the people from the other extreme – those who seemed to have things much better than she did. 'It's the easy option to drift into bitterness,' she says. 'It was easy to look at friends and think, "It's all right for them – they've had a family exactly to plan." But for how long will it be all right for them? Something could go wrong at any time.

'So often the object of your grief can become dislodged and you resent other people. But you can't live life like that. I had to decide *not* to live life like that.

'I believe God gave me the dignity to carry on, and to be able to hold other people's babies in public. I made a conscious decision that I wasn't going to avoid friends having babies, or to avoid their babies when they were born, because I didn't want to frighten them. It was difficult initially. In such a big church, there are always pregnant women. One friend had a baby boy at the same time as one of mine would have been born, and there were constant reminders. But I enjoyed seeing him growing up, and I didn't feel bitter.

'Living through the miscarriages has been the most profound experience of my life,' she says. 'But who knows what lies ahead?'

David agrees. He says the experience was unforgettable, and that's the way it should be. But he has now accepted it as another milestone in life's experience. 'We will never forget the babies we never saw,' he says. 'But life goes on. You have to pick up whatever pieces are lying around, and get on with it.

'I'm sure there are other things that lie ahead that will be an even greater challenge to our emotions. I don't think we'll look back on the miscarriages as the greatest challenge. But they'll always be there, and they may give the grounding and stability to cope with whatever lies ahead.'

5

Another wave of grief

Five years after they were married, Vernon and Christine decided it was time to start a family. It was 1984, and Christine would have liked to have started her first baby before her thirtieth birthday the following year.

But eighteen months later, when she had still not become pregnant, the couple sought specialist help. After tests, they were told that Vernon's sperm count was very low, and it was highly unlikely they would ever be able to have children.

Coming to terms with this news added to the stress they were already feeling. Vernon was working as a curate in Sheffield, and although they were happy with the congregation at their church, there were many problems and difficulties among the leadership. When the Bishop wanted them to move on to an inner-city church, they realised they couldn't cope with that sort of life at that time. Vernon started to look around for other posts, and in October 1987, whilst writing a book for them, he began work for a publisher in the south of England.

Christine ran her own translation business in partnership with colleagues in Sheffield, and she wanted to continue with her work. So the search was on for a suitable place to live, within commuting distance of their two jobs. One house sale fell through, but they eventually moved to a Midlands market town in January 1988.

Life was very full as they settled into their changed way of life. They found a new church and friends; Vernon adapted to his new role and career, and they both got used to travelling to their jobs. They had also started to get used to the idea that they would not have children of their own. The option of IVF had been discussed and rejected – even though a parishioner from their Sheffield church had offered to pay for the treatment. Adoption was still a possibility, but Christine in particular wasn't keen to go ahead. They felt fortunate to have each other, and to have work they enjoyed. Life started to fit into a pattern – without children.

So it was an understatement to say they were surprised when, ten months after their move, Christine found she was pregnant. Vernon says he felt like Abraham in Genesis 17 and 18 – although he wasn't quite so old! They had been trying for a baby for almost five years, and it was three years since they had been told they wouldn't have children.

At the beginning of the pregnancy, someone gave her what purported to be a word of knowledge, from Isaiah 40:11, 'He will gather the lambs in his arms, he will carry them in his bosom, and gently lead those that are with young.'

The pregnancy wasn't easy. Not only did Christine suffer badly from oedema – 'I looked like an elephant!' she laughs – but she also had gestational diabetes. In July 1989, they went to their house in York (bought as an investment for retirement when Vernon had entered the ministry) for a fortnight's holiday. On the morning of Sunday 16 July, one month before the baby was due, Christine's membranes ruptured.

Vernon took her to York District Hospital, where, four hours later, her labour was induced. It lasted only three hours and forty-two minutes, with the baby being helped out with forceps at the end. The little boy weighed 5lb 4oz, and rated high on the Apgar score. But as a precaution he was taken to Special Care for observation, partly because he was one month premature, and also because a mother's gestational diabetes can affect the baby.

He was eight days old before his parents finally decided on his name. They particularly wanted the name to be special, as a way of saying thank you to God. So they were stuck between Samuel, meaning 'blessed by God', and Jonathan, which means 'gift of God'. At last they decided on Jonathan Mark.

Jonathan was kept in Special Care, even after Christine had been discharged from the hospital. The staff said he was rather slow and sleepy, and not responding well to outside influences. But he had begun to feed, and appeared to Christine and Vernon to be thriving. They felt fairly easy about his health, as the care was excellent.

On the eighth day, Monday, Christine spent all day with Jonathan in Special Care. 'He was so lively, and there was so much hope,' she remembers. But on the evening of that same day, when Vernon went to visit Jonathan, the paediatric consultant approached him. He said he was beginning to suspect that Jonathan was suffering from a constriction of one of the major arteries (coarctation of the aorta). A baby can survive with that condition for seven to ten days, but after that the temporary duct from the lungs to the heart, which is part of the baby's circulation system before birth, closes down, and the aorta normally takes over. In Jonathan's case, the duct was closing down, but the aorta didn't appear to be taking over.

Jonathan would have to be taken to Leeds the next day for further tests, the consultant, Dr Harran, advised. And if his suspicions were correct, the baby would need an operation. Dr Harran explained everything thoroughly, even giving Vernon a chart, showing the development of the heart and lungs, to take home to Christine.

Dr Harran assured Vernon and Christine that the heart surgeon in Leeds was the best. He would have no hesitation in referring his own children to him, if he ever needed to. But he warned them that the surgeon's manner was brusque, and they shouldn't be too distressed by it. 'This proved to be an understatement,' says Vernon.

By this time, Vernon and Christine had had to move out of their house in York, having previously arranged that friends could borrow the house for a holiday. After all, they had expected to stay only a fortnight before returning home to await the arrival of their baby. Now they were committed to stay in York until Jonathan was discharged, so they moved across the road to stay in a neighbour's empty house. They say they will never forget the blue front door and the knock.

At eight-thirty the next morning, when Vernon and Christine were having breakfast prior to leaving for the hospital, there was a sudden banging on the door. A young and inexperienced policeman told them simply, 'Your baby's deteriorated – you've got to go to the hospital straight away.' There was no phone in the house, and the hospital had been unable to contact them any other way.

Arriving at the hospital in a terrible state of shock, they found Jonathan on a ventilator, wrapped in blankets in an incubator. He had had an apnoea attack that morning, and had stopped breathing for a short time. The chaplain was waiting for them.

'He asked us if we wanted the baby christened,' says Christine. 'It made me so angry – it seemed to indicate that this was the end. I said we weren't giving up hope, Jonathan would be baptised in front of the whole church. And if he really was so ill, all we needed to do was go to Leeds, where he could have his operation.'

Vernon and Christine watched Jonathan being 'loaded' into the ambulance with Marion, the nursing sister who had been responsible for him. They followed in the car to Leeds. He was admitted into an intensive care ward where, along with other babies, he was stretched out on to what looked like an architect's drawing-board, heated by an infra-red light from above, tubes coming at him from all directions. 'The babies looked as if they were all pegged out,' says Vernon. 'It was heart-rending.'

A scan confirmed that Jonathan was suffering from coarctation of the aorta. The surgeon who was to perform the operation came to speak to Vernon and Christine. 'The great man approached, complete with silk bow-tie,' remembers Vernon. 'He was arrogant and self-assured – though, we were told, brilliant. He told us he had a ninety-six per cent success rate with this operation. It couldn't be done immediately because they had to stabilise Jonathan's condition first. We were told to go, and come back at seven o'clock.'

The couple got through the day somehow – although they only have two clear memories of what they did during that time. They went to a church in a small village, and knelt to pray for Jonathan at the communion rail. There was no sense of panic – hadn't they just been reassured of a ninety-six per cent success rate? Then they had a pub lunch, and Christine says she can even now taste the cold chips she almost choked on there.

Arriving back at the hospital at seven o'clock, they found that Jonathan had had one operation. But they were told nothing else, and were just asked to sit in the waiting-room. While they waited they phoned Christine's father and two close friends, one from their old church in Sheffield and one from their new church. Immediately, these friends contacted others from both churches, and two groups met to pray.

At eight thirty, the surgeon came out of the operating theatre and met Vernon and Christine in the corridor. He said to them, 'This is one of the poorliest babies I've ever seen. I'm going to have to operate again.' And then he left them.

Vernon's legs gave way, and he began to reel down the corridor. Christine, furious at being told the news in the corridor, managed to help him back into the waiting-room, where he started to retch over the sink. The waiting-room was hot and stuffy; they went outside. 'Vernon ranted and raved round the flower beds,' says Christine. 'I'd never seen him like that before – it was one of the hardest things to bear. I went back inside and rang my friends and father again – I needed someone to explode to.'

Back in the waiting-room, they stared at the TV, trying to concentrate and block out thought. Then at nine thirty, they were called into the sister's office, and asked to sit down. The consultant came in, said, 'I'm terribly sorry, your baby's dead,' and left the room.

'I was really angry,' says Christine. 'I wanted to know why, and I wanted to know exactly what had happened. I demanded to see someone who had been in the operating theatre. We were taken into one of those clinical, emotionally-removed rooms, with abstract pictures on the walls and easy chairs and tables around. Someone brought in tea and toast. We wanted to fling the jam-pot at the walls. I said I wanted to see Jonathan. The sister eventually brought him, wrapped in a shawl. She sat rocking him, cooing over him as if he were alive – it was very distressing. Then we held him ourselves. A young surgeon came in and asked us what we wanted to know. He sat cross-legged on the floor and answered all our questions.

'There were so many emotions in such a small amount of time, you can't take it in,' Christine continues. 'On the previous Sunday night at communion I'd been overwhelmed with gratitude, and only forty-eight hours later there was total devastation. None of it made *any* sense.'

Christine phoned the friends who were praying, to tell them Jonathan had died. Their vicar, Mike, and his wife drove straight up from the Midlands, arriving at the hospital at midnight. They saw Jonathan, then drove Christine and Vernon back to their neighbour's house in York.

The next day, Mike crossed the road to ask the friends who were using Christine and Vernon's house if, in the circumstances, they could vacate it. Then the couple went to York District Hospital to deal with the paperwork involved in a death. A midwife offered to do Christine's post-natal check there and then, so that she wouldn't have to bother with it when she got home. 'She took me to a room, lay down on the bed with me and sobbed with me,' says Christine. 'We have nothing but praise for the way we were treated in that hospital – particularly the Special Care Baby Unit. The care was superb.

'Similarly, the funeral directors were sympathetic yet very professional. Those early days were almost easier than later. Though the visits to the undertaker's and to the registrar were difficult, we were supported by caring people and the shock numbed the agony.'

The couple went for lunch in a pub on the North Yorkshire moors, to plan the funeral. Christine remembers Vernon breaking down, saying, 'I never thought I'd be sitting here planning my own son's funeral.' As a clergyman, he had arranged many others – but this was so appallingly different.

'There followed numb days when we seemed "all right",' says Vernon. They say they haven't a clue what they did for the rest of the week while they waited in York for the funeral.

Only one clear memory emerges. Vernon's sister brought his mother up from the West Country; Vernon and Christine met them at the station, and took them to the hotel where they were to stay. Jonathan's death was hardly mentioned. Vernon's sister said it was 'too distressing for Mum', so they shouldn't dwell on it. When they reached the hotel, mother and sister produced their holiday snaps, and expected Christine and Vernon to be interested. Vernon says, 'It was just as though a pet guinea-pig had died.' And after the funeral, on the way from the hotel to the station, Vernon's mother asked for the car to stop so she could buy her neighbour a present from York – as if she had come up for a holiday.

In contrast, when Christine's father arrived for the funeral, he was devastated, and could only say how sorry he was.

The funeral was held on 31 July at St Michael le Belfrey, a church they often attended when in York. Christine and Vernon felt they couldn't bear to bring the tiny body back to a town where they had lived for only eighteen months and which had no emotional ties for them. But they did ask Mike, their vicar, to give the address. The vicar of St Michael's presided over the funeral and burial. The couple found his support, although he didn't know them, was warm and practical.

About eighty people attended the service, many of them from the couple's old church in Sheffield. The coffin had already been placed at the front of the church, with the flowers on the top tied in a huge ribbon. At the beginning of the service, Jane, a good friend, placed Vernon and Christine's simple bouquet on the coffin. Jane was pregnant, and the contrast between new life and death was poignant.

Jonathan was buried in a cemetery on the outskirts of York. Jane's parents from the Sheffield church organised tea for family at the house afterwards.

On 1 August, Vernon and Christine returned home. The paediatric consultant, Dr Harran, had suggested they ask for genetic counselling, since what had happened to Jonathan could happen again and they needed to know what the chances were. When Christine rang the surgery to cancel her next, now unnecessary, ante-natal appointment, she was put through to the health visitor, who, it turned out, was also the genetic link-nurse. The nurse, Liz, said she was about to go on holiday for ten days, but would see Christine and Vernon when she returned.

The next Sunday evening, the couple's GP visited them, after having preached at his own church. 'He spent most of the time sorting out his own theological problems about what had happened,' says Vernon. 'He wanted answers. But I knew from my own work that there *were* no answers – and yet here was this doctor trying to work out his own theology of suffering in my lounge. I wanted to get a pile of books on suffering from the attic and pass them on to him, and say, "Come back when you've read that lot."

'He was the first of many who upset us because they wanted to work the problem out for themselves, to know where *they* stood,' he continues. 'Some people can't cope with the loose ends – it's too painful for them not to have answers.

'Inevitably our image of God is in part a reflection of our own needs and wants. But this is idolatry: making false images of God. It's also psychologically damaging if we tell people that God works it out in such-and-such a way (because we'd like to believe that he does), when in reality he has not promised to do so.

'It's a bit like teenagers and guidance,' Vernon explains. 'A teenager often develops a strong belief in guidance. They desperately want answers to their all-too-human teenage insecurity, so they demand that God guides them. I've given more talks on guidance than I care to think.

'But the danger is that a teenager expects certain things of God (in terms of miraculous signs and guidance) that God has not promised to provide. So, too, many adult Christians fear not knowing the answers. And because they want a purpose for everything, because they want to feel secure, they invent a theology in which everything all works to plan. They forget that the Bible also talks about evil thwarting God's purpose, or human free will.

'My own intellectual uncertainty had now become sharpened with emotional pain,' he says.

Vernon spent over three hours each day commuting to and from his office. Added to his working day, it meant he was out of the house for at least twelve hours, so was not there to support Christine. He tried to work at home, but the company weren't happy about it.

The most devastating thing for Christine to cope with, as she sat alone during the long days, was the feeling that she'd had her chance, and lost it. They had been told they would be childless, then they'd been given Jonathan – and now they'd lost him. They had felt like Abraham and Sarah – but now what?

'Our anger and frustration put into question the Isaiah 40 word of knowledge,' says Christine. 'If that was genuine, had God changed his mind? The church had been so positive, people had said we could trust God, Jonathan would be all right, because he was a miracle. So the shock produced an angry reaction against the church, because we felt they'd misled us. And I felt angry because I'd *allowed* myself to be misled.

'I felt very angry with God, too. It's cruel that you wait so long for a child and then watch as it dies. It's worse than not having had a child in the first place. One friend kept reiterating, "At least you're a mother now." Well, biologically, yes – but emotionally? I was not a mother in the real sense of caring for and seeing my child grow up.

The only hymns they could relate to were the Victorian ones. 'The Victorians knew about suffering, death and loss, and it's reflected in the hymns – not like the modern triumphalist choruses,' says Vernon.

They met a mixture of responses. One work colleague of Vernon's never mentioned it, and hasn't to the present day. Others approached them with their own stories of loss, identifying with their grief. They found out that similar experiences had happened to people they'd known for years, but who had never mentioned it before. 'People crawl out of the woodwork when they know you've been there too,' says Christine.

Yet people who had themselves lost children were not usually the most helpful to them. One woman at church, whose own older child had died previously, attempted to counsel them. 'She gave us the "set patter" about trusting God,' says Christine. 'She came prepared with it, dished it out and then left without listening or asking any questions. I was amazed and appalled at how she appeared to have buried her own experience.'

'Many people who hadn't gone through anything like this experience didn't put a foot wrong,' says Vernon. 'Yet people are often scared of opening their mouths because they may say something wrong.'

'But saying nothing is worse,' says Christine. 'A simple "I'm *so* sorry" is all that's needed – it breaks the ice without embarrassment.'

One member of the church said how wonderful she thought Jonathan's funeral service had been. 'I said "No, it was awful," ' says Christine. 'She said we'd done all we could for him. Yes, we'd planned it well – but I didn't want someone to tell me it was lovely, like a praise service. I'd wanted to scream all the way through it, but felt too numb and weary to rebel!'

'The church didn't allow us to be Job-like,' says Vernon. 'There were more than two hundred people praying for Jonathan, and he still died. Why couldn't we ask, "Why me?"? God seemed to have turned his back on us.'

There were only a very few people that Vernon and Christine could allow near them in those early days. There were occasions when people from church came to see them, but would be turned away. 'At times we couldn't face others,' says Vernon. 'So people felt rejected – which they were – but if we turned them away once, they never tried again. They ditched us.'

They felt many in the church avoided them because they upset the theological balance. 'This just wasn't supposed to happen – particularly to leaders,' says Vernon. But they were determined to keep going to church, because their personal faith, in terms of reading and praying at home, had gone. 'So our lifeline was the corporate,' he says. 'If we couldn't pray, at least we could be part of a group that did. If we couldn't worship, at least we could remain in touch with those who could.'

A few close friends from the church, however, were very supportive. 'They struggled and suffered alongside us,' says Vernon. One friend, Hazel, had actually been praying a prayer of faith for Jonathan's healing at the exact minute Christine phoned to say he had died. When she heard the phone, Hazel had thought it was to say Jonathan was recovering.

'Hazel's faith took an enormous battering because of that,' says Vernon. 'She had the same questions as we did. What sort of God was he? We had been taught that all we had to do was ask, and the victory was ours.'

Liz, the genetic counsellor, returned from her holiday and started home visits. 'From August to February she came once a fortnight,' says Christine. 'She made sure we were the last appointment in the day, so she could stay as long as we needed her. She did classic non-directive counselling; she didn't tell us what to believe, but just listened and helped us explore it. There were never any answers from Liz, although she put things into context for us. She pointed out that some friends couldn't cope with us because they'd seen us as strong, they were relying on us being strong, and we'd cracked.

'It worried me that I talked so much to Liz, while Vernon had no one,' Christine continues. But Vernon says that although he spent less time talking to Liz, he too benefited from her help. 'She's the only one I've related to in all this,' he says. 'She was more helpful than the Christian "counsellors". Christians seemed to need to defend the Church or God; Liz allowed us to express our anger and doubts.'

Christine now, with hindsight, believes one friend at church who was trying to help her found it threatening that she was seeing so much of Liz. 'I wasn't able to let that friend near me – but at the same time I needed Liz to really help me. My friend felt we'd be wrongly influenced. I can understand we were in a vulnerable condition – but Liz was a professional who understood our vulnerability and never once put her own side of things. We didn't discover her own personal lack of faith until much later.'

Christine's relationship with her friend deteriorated. She had eventually gone back to work in October, having previously lost all confidence in her career, which wasn't helped by having three months off. But shortly before Christmas, she managed to finish a huge translation assignment, and felt the need of a celebration. So she visited her friend to suggest they went out for a coffee. Afterwards, they went back to the friend's house for a sherry.

'While I was there, I started to feel more and more uncomfortable,' says Christine. 'At first I didn't know why, but then I realised she was trying to counsel me, and I just had to leave. That night I couldn't sleep, I was in such distress. I just wanted to get on the motorway, and drive and drive. Maybe she thought, as a close Christian friend, that she ought to be able to help, or that the church expected her to take on that role. Certainly she seemed jealous that Liz had got the counselling job.

'I couldn't work out why I felt so terrible. I couldn't sleep. Later, we tried to sort things out, and I realised I'd been trying to avoid her. But then she started to get angry with Vernon, because she said he never showed his feelings. Vernon felt he was being asked to jump through hoops he didn't want to jump through, and he certainly didn't want to be rebuked for not expressing his feelings when the feelings were all so raw.'

Christine found she couldn't 'lose' herself in anything after Jonathan died. 'I was really *jealous* because Vernon could read five-hundred-page novels in order to lose himself,' she remembers. 'Even reading cards and letters of sympathy was a chore. Liz told us not to worry about it, and just to leave them until later. The best card we received just read "We're very sorry. All our love . . ." from friends who'd lost a baby at six months old. That one card said it all.'

'We needed to know we weren't alone, that we hadn't been isolated and picked out for this punishment,' says Christine. It helped her to watch traumatic TV programmes about couples and babies who had gone through similar experiences – although Vernon couldn't watch them at all. 'Yet when we heard about SANDS (Stillbirth and Neonatal Death Society), Vernon in particular didn't want to contact them, or to have to prop up anyone else. Having Liz was enough.'

In February 1990, Christine discovered she was pregnant again. Her first reaction was shock – she had thought Jonathan was her 'only chance'. With hindsight, if the couple had known they could conceive again, they say they would have waited longer, giving themselves more time to grieve for Jonathan.

But as well as the shock, Christine says she was also 'thrilled, and worried sick'. They decided not to tell people, as they wanted to come to terms with the pregnancy, and its implications. And there would have to be tests.

Jonathan's post-mortem had shown that part of his heart was missing (diagnosis: 'markedly hypoplastic aortic arch') so when his full circulation started after the operation, his heart couldn't cope with it. Christine and Vernon had been told by the genetic consultant in Birmingham that there was a one in fifty chance of Jonathan's condition recurring in any future children.

They were offered an early scan at the local hospital. At eleven weeks, the scan showed no problems with the baby's heart. Climbing down from the couch, Christine, who was much bigger at eleven weeks than she had been at that stage of her first pregnancy, asked if that was normal in a second pregnancy.

The radiographer said it wasn't, and suggested Christine should climb back up so she could take a second look. Then she said, 'Oh yes, there's another one hiding behind this one!'

Christine burst into tears. The radiographer told her to pull herself together and be positive – it wasn't as bad as all that! 'And she still had my ante-natal notes from Jonathan in her hand!' says Christine.

Christine, crying and feeling devastated, phoned Vernon at work. He came home and they phoned Liz, who visited the house. Liz, although she was also shocked by their news, was still able to point out some positive things about having twins – they would always have a playmate, and they wouldn't be lonely.

A less helpful comment came from a member of the church, who when she found out about the twins said, 'God's sent you two babies to make up for having lost one.' Christine felt, 'She was just dismissing Jonathan, and suggesting he could be compensated for, as if one person can just replace another.'

Some weeks later, feeling anxious about the babies, Christine felt she had to have a detailed cardiac scan to ensure both their hearts were healthy. But the obstetrician at her local hospital refused. With the support of Liz and her GP, Christine managed to book another scan at Birmingham. At twenty-two weeks, the scan was inconclusive, and she was booked in again two weeks later.

At the twenty-four week scan, the cardiologist pronounced the hearts healthy. But the consultant radiologist pointed out the large amount of fluid in the amniotic sac around one twin. There was one placenta for both babies, and one twin was attached to the middle of it, while the smaller twin was on the edge. The big twin was preventing most of the nutrients going to the little twin and was also producing an excessive amount of fluid. There was twin-to-twin transfusion.

'We didn't find out until afterwards that it was their way of saying there were complications and we might lose one or both twins,' says Vernon.

They were referred back to their local hospital, where they had an appointment at twenty-seven weeks. 'The consultant obstetrician there just dismissed it,' says Christine. 'He suggested bed rest, and said he'd take me in at thirty-two weeks. We had resisted early admission to hospital – which we wouldn't have done if we'd been told the dangers. But we thought it would be less stressful if I rested at home, where friends could visit whenever they liked. We also needed to be with each other.'

Vernon is very angry that the possible outcome of the pregnancy was not explained to them. 'No one told us this is the problem, this may happen, this is how you prepare,' he says.

Five days later, Christine walked about four hundred yards to the post office. She felt something wasn't right, and returning home she found she had had a slight 'show'. She went straight to bed, and stayed there throughout the rest of the day and that night. At seven o'clock the next morning, as Vernon was about to leave for work in London, Christine had a larger show of mucus and asked him to ring the hospital.

He was told to bring her straight in, and although Christine was frightened that her waters might break she had to walk down the stairs and, on reaching the local hospital, had to walk to the maternity ward. There, while she was being examined, she felt the trickle start.

There was suddenly a great deal of activity – although Christine and Vernon weren't made aware of what was going on. In the background, phone calls were being made to most of the large hospitals in the Midlands – and even as far south as Oxford, with the possibility being discussed of Christine being sent there by helicopter!

At last twin cots were found to be available in New Cross Hospital, Wolverhampton, and Christine was wheeled into an ambulance, along with a district midwife, two paramedics, a registrar – and two cots. Vernon, who hadn't been told where the ambulance was going, chased behind in the car. Worrying about what was going on in the ambulance, he tried to keep up with it as it rushed up the motorway, sirens screaming and lights flashing. A police car met them at the Wolverhampton exit and escorted them to the hospital.

It was still only 9.30 a.m. when the ambulance reached the hospital. The consultant paediatrician was waiting for them, and he assured everyone, 'We'll look after her, don't worry.' Christine was taken to the delivery room, but as there were no contractions she was moved down to the ward. And there she and Vernon waited, in a hot ante-natal ward, watching Wimbledon on the television.

By 5.03 p.m., while she was drinking coffee, Christine was experiencing horrendous cramps in her legs. Crawling round the bed, she knocked the coffee over, and a panicking nurse, believing her waters had finally broken, had Christine sent back to the delivery room. There, the 'old school' consultant kept Vernon out of the room; he was eventually told that the labour had started and what the consultant proposed doing.

At nine o'clock, the smaller twin's feet were visible; it was breech. A decision was quickly taken to do an emergency Caesarian section under general anaesthetic. 'The staff were wonderful – so fast – they said, "Don't worry, we'll get them out!" ' remembers Christine.

The twin girls were born at 9.24 and 9.27 p.m. on 26 June 1990. Hannah weighed just under 2lb; Claire was a mere 15oz. They were wrapped in foil and rushed to Intensive Care. As they were pushed past Vernon, a nurse called, 'If you want to see your babies, look now,' and he just caught sight of two tiny heads.

When Christine came round, Vernon was sitting by her side. She vaguely remembers him telling her they had two little girls, and asking him if they were all right. On hearing they were, she told him to go home and get some rest.

Vernon did leave – but not to go home. Feeling the need of company, he went to see Liz and her husband, and had just a little too much to drink. He found that Liz already knew about the panic of that morning. She had happened to arrive at the local hospital just as Christine was being whisked away in the ambulance, and had made enquiries. She had been told 'it doesn't look good', so was relieved when Vernon was able to tell her that both twins had survived the birth.

The next thing Christine was aware of, in her post-operative stupor, was a voice asking, 'Can you hear me?' The consultant paediatrician went on, 'We're wondering where your husband is?'

The staff wanted to use Surfactant to lubricate the babies' lungs, and needed the permission of a parent. Christine didn't need to refer them to Vernon: she just said, 'Yes, do anything you can to save them.'

Then it was the next morning, and Christine woke to find Mike, their vicar, sitting by her bed. It was the first of his visits; he continued to drive up to the hospital every day, but Christine says, 'We shut him out. We couldn't deal with someone else's panic and questions, and I was still drifting in and out of consciousness after the previous twenty-four hours, and being sick from the after-effects of the anaesthetic.'

Mike told Christine that the staff wanted her to go up and see the twins. 'I didn't want to,' she says. 'I didn't want to invest emotion and hope in them. I told Mike that I'd wait for Vernon.' And when Vernon arrived, later that morning, the couple went together to look at the babies.

'We knew deep down their chances of survival were minimal,' says Vernon. So it was almost without a sense of shock that they received the news, the following morning, that Hannah was dying. But the consultant paediatrician was terribly shocked and upset when she told them. Hannah, the bigger twin, had had the greater chance of survival, and she couldn't understand why she was dying.

Vernon and Christine went back to Intensive Care, where Vernon baptised first Hannah and then Claire. 'It was different this time,' says Christine. 'We hadn't wanted Jonathan baptised because we thought there'd be a church welcome. Baptism is all about belonging to a Christian community, and makes most sense in the context of a local church service. But with the twins, we knew this was the end.' After she was baptised, there was no point putting Hannah back in the incubator, and Vernon continued to hold her. At thirty-six hours old, she died.

Throughout that day and the next, Christine dreaded hearing the footsteps approaching her room, bringing someone to tell her the worst about Claire. Although so tiny, the little twin was a real fighter and was struggling for life.

'I kept going to see Claire,' says Christine. 'I realised that, however short her life was going to be, I had to be there for her.'

It was late afternoon on the day after Hannah died that the footsteps Christine dreaded came to her door. Vernon and Christine went straight to Intensive Care, and Claire was taken out of her incubator. They were both able to hold her, and take photographs. Christine was holding her when she died, at three days old.

The twins' post-mortem would later reveal that they had no physical defect. Their deaths were due to 'extreme prematurity'.

The hospital chaplain, Derek, came to visit them. They found his attitude refreshing. 'He didn't give us any woolly answers or wrapped-up clichés to the questions we asked him,' says Vernon. 'He just said, "I don't know," and "Suffering is part of our evil world." '

'And he summed the situation up in a nutshell,' adds Christine. 'He said, "We have to believe that Hannah and Claire have gone to a better world – but that doesn't make it any easier for those who are left behind." '

'The sense of death and afterlife being part of daily life is taboo, not to be discussed, in the Church,' says Vernon. 'But the Bible doesn't say that.'

It was only eleven months after Jonathan's death, and they felt they couldn't go through with another big funeral service. Added to this, Christine says the twins' death felt like a 'horrendous miscarriage' in comparison to Jonathan's death – she hadn't bonded with them in the same way. So they decided on a private ceremony at the hospital chapel and then the crematorium. The two tiny coffins travelled to the crematorium on the front seat of Derek's car, and only Derek, Vernon and Christine attended the ten-minute funeral. 'It was so different to Jonathan's funeral, where we were surrounded by friends,' says Vernon. 'Here we were alone in a hospital chapel, without even a member of staff in attendance.'

Later, Vernon and Christine collected the twins' ashes. They had originally asked for permission to open Jonathan's grave in York, so the twins' bodies could be buried with their brother's, but it was apparently 'against health regulations'. The authorities did, however, agree that the twins' ashes could be put in Jonathan's grave.

'It was ironic that none of the clergy at York could take the service because they were all at a Wimber healing conference,' says

Vernon. 'So a work colleague of mine took a short service at the grave. Christine's father came down, and then the four of us went for coffee at a hotel near the cemetery.'

Vernon returned to work almost straight away. 'I wanted to be at home,' he says. 'But I felt guilty. When you work for a Christian organisation, it's like a mission. I felt I had to go in.'

'My boss had told me to "take as much time as you need". And my GP had asked if I wanted to be signed off work. But I said, "I don't know." You can't ask those kinds of questions of a grieving person; you're not strong enough to make decisions. Today, I'd say, "Yes, of course I'll take time off," but I couldn't decide that then. When Jonathan died there were times I couldn't even decide what to buy as I wheeled my trolley around the supermarket. At times a grieving person needs help in making decisions.'

'If there was any problem between the two of us, it was that,' says Christine. 'I feel that family comes before work, even before deadlines.'

Yet the couple became even closer than they already were. Christine's father had said to them, 'You've got to cling to each other – the ultimate tragedy would be if you two split up.' And while they grieved in different ways, they learnt to respect that difference.

For some months, Christine suffered badly from depression. At the same time, Liz was ill, and Christine was unable to see her until the following October. During that time, she describes her friend Hazel as her 'lifeline'. Hazel phoned every day, and would often drive round to collect Christine and take her out. They would spend hours sitting in the garden at Hazel's house, talking and crying. 'She walked through it with me,' says Christine. 'And it's the greatest gift anyone can give you. That's what it means to lay down your life for someone.'

The GP referred her to a counsellor, but it didn't help much. Christine felt she was only attending the sessions to keep everyone else happy, and she eventually pulled out.

The grief they felt after Jonathan's death was now compounded. Yet Vernon feels their second bereavement was a continuation of the grief they were still feeling, rather than a worsening of it. 'After

Jonathan died,' he says, 'most days were dreadful, totally black, no colour left at all. And when the twins died, people said it must be horrendous to have another death. But it wasn't. It felt like just another wave of grief. But when you're almost drowned in the first, another wave is a continuation, not a catastrophe.'

Their doubts and questions were reinforced. Several people quoted Romans 8:28 to them: 'We know that all things work together for good to them that love God, to them who are the called according to his purpose.' They couldn't take it.

'They said there must be a reason for it,' says Christine. 'Some of these people had been through suffering themselves, but they'd put it in a slot marked: "God's purpose". I reacted in a totally different way, and we had nothing to say to each other. I can't see any purpose in it at all; there's nothing that comes out of it, except pain and damage.'

And Vernon adds, 'The New English Bible says that "*in* everything God works for good", that's a better way of understanding it. God is *in* every situation trying to redeem it, much as a parent cares for his or her child when they are hurting. But that is a million miles away from saying that a parent deliberately hurts a child *in order* to improve that child.'

The occasional cry Christine made to God was 'Help! – but you're not going to do anything anyway, so what's the point?' And she also asked, 'If God can heal, but he chooses not to, what's the point of having that power? And why should I be bothered anyway? What good has it done to be a Christian?

'I haven't totally lost my faith,' she goes on. 'But it's very different now. I'm a very different person. The basic roots of my faith are the cross and the resurrection, not triumphalism and victory. It's so difficult to be honest with many evangelicals; there no longer seems to be much interest in the pursuit of spiritual truth. They're not interested in whether healing really works or does take place. Triumphalism is the current craze. The emphasis of the Church is wrong – it should be the cross, every bit as much as the Holy Spirit.

'I still believe that God makes a difference to people's lives, and changes their attitudes. But I feel cheated. And what's the purpose of all the suffering endured by our close friends because of what has happened to us? It hasn't encouraged them – one of them nearly lost her faith through it. And it's made some of those close to us, who have been struggling to come to faith for years, now give up.'

Christine felt as if she was going mad, as both she and Vernon struggled with the intellectual and spiritual problems arising from what had happened to them. Vernon thought, 'Either my theology is totally wrong, or there is something in what I believe and the Church is peddling a cheap version of Christianity'.

Eventually, they decided to seek the help and advice of an internationally-respected Christian leader. He rebuked them for doubting God, but said yes, by all means doubt the words sometimes given by individuals in the church. He also told them that no one had the right to give individuals words of knowledge, like the Isaiah 40 word which had been given to them. 'We realised it was the church that had misled us, not God,' says Christine. 'God doesn't give promises like that.'

In the end, Christine feels they were left with two alternatives. 'We could give in to despair, or we could carry on and hope for something better. In reality, there was *no* choice.'

Vernon says they had anticipated the pain of grief, but what they hadn't expected were the power struggles, both in the church and in the hospitals. Power struggles and bureaucracy about which hospital they were allowed to go to, which consultant they could see, why they weren't allowed to see the notes regarding the twins. Power struggles in the church as to who should counsel them or who would be the one to 'really help them'.

Then in March 1991 Christine discovered she was pregnant again.

'I wanted to make a fresh start,' says Christine. 'We changed hospitals and towns, and were looked after by a marvellous, supportive consultant. He gave us so much confidence; he answered our questions, and told us everything that was happening.'

Despite the excellent care she received, Christine was still obviously worried about her baby. For the first six weeks she thought she would lose the baby, as she had continual bleeding. Her gestational diabetes was much worse than in her previous pregnancies, and at eighteen weeks she was put under the care of the diabetes consultant and had to follow a special diet. She was scanned every two weeks, and was incredibly relieved when all the scans were pronounced clear.

Towards the end of the pregnancy, the consultant said Christine should be admitted for bed rest, and, after much thought and discussion, an epidural Caesarean section was booked for thirty-nine weeks. But at 8.30 p.m. on the day before Christine was thirty-eight weeks, her waters broke. Her immediate reaction was panic; she couldn't stop shaking. She was wheeled to delivery, where because they were so busy, the consultant on duty suggested a general anaesthetic rather than an epidural section. Christine didn't mind. 'When it came to it, I just wanted the baby out, and well,' she says.

Kate was born at 11.46 p.m. on 5 November 1991. She weighed 7lb 11½oz. When Christine woke up she was in a bed in a corridor, and Vernon was holding her hand. 'We've got a beautiful baby daughter,' he told her.

Christine was wheeled down to the Special Care Unit, where Kate was put in her arms for a few minutes. The staff reassured her the baby was all right – it was just a precaution because of the gestational diabetes.

Kate was kept on a drip for sixteen hours because of a sugar imbalance, but at four the next afternoon she was brought to Christine's room. And that night, although the staff suggested the baby stayed in the nursery so Christine could rest, she needed to keep Kate close.

'That night, when I picked her up to feed her, we spent three-quarters of an hour just gazing at each other,' says Christine. 'I put my ear to her heart, and heard it beating. She looked *so* like Jonathan. But this time there was no ventilator, and no tubes. Just her and me.'

When Kate was five days old, Christine and Vernon took her home. 'I remember crying, driving home in the car, because we hadn't done this before,' says Christine. 'We sat at home that night, numb with emotion, watching TV.'

For the next three months Christine says she was 'in a terrible state', terrified that Kate was going to die. But she was perfectly healthy – until at fifteen months she was admitted to hospital for a week with pneumonia. Christine spent the whole time in tears, but found she was removing herself emotionally from the situation. She was unable to stay with Kate overnight at the hospital, where the smell and the noise were so evocative of the deaths of her other babies.

'I've struggled with myself since having Kate,' says Christine. 'Because of the way I loved her, I felt sure I wouldn't lose my temper with her. But when I'm under stress and tired, I do – and I feel so guilty. I remember one afternoon, when she was five weeks old, she wouldn't stop crying, and I felt like throwing her through the window. I had to phone Vernon at work and ask him to come home.'

And Vernon adds, 'I don't think we're better parents because of what we've been through. We've not "recovered"; we don't feel strong. You'd think, all these years after Jonathan died, and after all we've been through, that molehills would *be* molehills. But no. When we moved house recently it was a huge thing. We realised that we're not "better" yet. Stronger, yes – but not strong.'

Kate is a special baby to her parents' old friends from their church in Sheffield. They take an active interest in her, and send presents at every opportunity. And the past is not kept secret from Kate. At the age of two, she is able to identify her baby brother from his photographs.

Christine and Vernon feel there has been light at the end of their dark tunnel because of Kate. But at the same time, if Kate hadn't been born, Christine says she would see life as very dark and painful. 'What would be the point?' she asks. 'Coming to terms with infertility was one thing, it was loss. But once you've tasted what it's like to have a baby, and it's gone – that's another thing altogether.'

She says she has lost all enthusiasm for involvement in church life and evangelism. 'I've got nothing to say,' she admits. 'I can be enthusiastic for Christian projects in the developing world, or for Special Care babies. But my black-and-white evangelistic faith has gone.'

Vernon says he can't pray on a 'petty' scale any more. He says he rejoices in being an Anglican, because it enables him to go through the motions even when his heart isn't in it.

But he says that while he doesn't have answers, he still feels that God was with him through the suffering. 'He was alongside me and he bothers with me. He suffered too. The God we worship identifies with our pain. He is a God of the cross, and that keeps me believing. Just.'

6

'Nothing shall separate us . . .'

Chris and Jane's only son was nearly two years old when Jane
became pregnant for the second time. In January 1984, just after
Kevin's second birthday party, when Jane was fifteen weeks pregnant, she began to feel ill. She felt very tired – the mothers of the
other children at the party told her she looked drained. When she
began to feel sick, she thought she'd contracted food poisoning.

The following day was Sunday, and the family went to church
as usual. But after lunch Jane started to be violently sick every
half hour, and had dreadful stomach pain. She still thought it was
something she'd eaten, and she went to bed, leaving Chris to look
after Kevin. By midnight, when she was rolling in agony, Chris
phoned the night-duty doctor.

'Gastroenteritis,' said the doctor, giving her some medication.
But the pain became worse, and she continued to be sick throughout
the night. She sent Chris into the spare bedroom, feeling she
was disturbing him too much.

The next morning she visited her own doctor. He agreed with
the gastroenteritis diagnosis and sent her home with painkillers,
saying he would come out to her if she was no better. As the
day progressed, she felt even worse. That evening Chris phoned
the doctor, and was told to phone again in the morning if things
had not improved.

They did not improve. After a terrible night, Chris decided to
take the morning off work, and the doctor was summoned. Chris
also phoned Jane's mum, who could look after Kevin so Chris
could go to work in the afternoon. The doctor examined Jane,

and immediately phoned the hospital and demanded a bed, even though there 'wasn't one available'. After calling an ambulance, he sat with Jane, holding her hand.

Now the question was – could Jane's mum go to hospital with her, or must she stay to look after Kevin? At that point the telephone rang. It was Helen, a friend of Jane's, who had felt prompted to ring although she didn't know why. She immediately came round to care for Kevin, freeing Jane's mum to go to hospital.

Jane can hardly remember the trip to hospital; she was terribly dehydrated and was drifting in and out of sleep. She can just remember being lifted into the ambulance by wheelchair, and being taken into the maternity ward at the hospital.

'There seemed to be lots of doctors, and they kept asking me questions about what I'd eaten,' she recalls. 'Two of them still said it was a gastric problem. I don't know what the others said.'

Jane was put on a drip, had blood tests, had her blood pressure monitored – and still couldn't even keep water down. The blood tests showed nothing wrong. Two days later she was taken for a scan – but of the gall-bladder rather than the womb, a fact which she still can't understand. The scan showed no gall-bladder problems.

After three days in the maternity wing, Jane was feeling better and asked to go home. Although she had her own room, she could still hear the cries of new-born babies. Feeling confused and having no idea what was happening to her, she found the sounds upsetting. But she was told she must stay in hospital over the weekend.

On Sunday and Monday Jane noticed her blood pressure was being checked much more frequently. But she felt well, and on Monday morning she went to chat with some of the new mums in the ward. She found it very frustrating to be told she was on her feet too much, and must have bed rest.

Meanwhile, family and friends were rallying round. Friends from church kept up with the washing, ironing and cooking. Kevin was being cared for by a succession of grandparents and friends, and was brought to the hospital each day to visit his mother. Other visitors were not always welcome. Jane remembers that

'Some delightful "friends" said I'd been doing too much, and others said it was psychosomatic.'

But one welcome visitor was John, the vicar from the family's church. He arrived for his regular visit before lunch on the Monday, when Jane had been sent back to bed to rest. 'I was really fed up,' says Jane. 'I'd been in hospital nearly a week, I felt fine, and they were making me stay in bed. I just felt it wasn't fair. John managed to calm me down.'

After John left, Jane was taken for a scan. It was an alarming experience.

'The woman who was scanning me just stood silently, looking at the screen. Then she turned everything off and said she was going for the doctor. I lay on my own for what seemed like ages, but it may only have been a few minutes.

'When she came back with the doctor, she turned the machine on again, and they both stared at it. I asked them to tell me what was happening, but the doctor only said he'd have to talk to my consultant. I said I'd got a right to know, but he said my own doctor would tell me. And I was taken back to the ward.'

That Monday afternoon, when Jane's in-laws brought Kevin for his daily visit, a blood-pressure test had just given a very high reading. A nurse had given her valium to bring the blood pressure down.

'It knocked me out – I just wanted to sleep,' says Jane. 'I had to ask Chris's parents to take Kevin home. Half of me felt guilty because I wasn't giving him time, but the other half was really worried about what was happening to me.'

The next thing Jane was aware of was her consultant standing by her bed. 'I expect you're wondering what's going on?' he said. Jane agreed that she was, rather, yes.

'Your scan showed something quite unusual, but we have to take more blood tests to confirm it,' he went on. He explained that she had a hydatidiform mole, a tumour which affects the membrane surrounding the baby, and prevents its development. The condition is rare; the last time the hospital had seen it was eight years before. If the blood tests confirmed the diagnosis, Jane would have to have an abortion.

'Then curtains were drawn around my bed, and I was left alone,' said Jane. 'I didn't know whether to cry or not. A friend arrived to visit me – and that was it. I let it all out.'

She felt terribly frightened about what was happening. Everything seemed out of her control. The whole situation was so unreal, and there wasn't enough time to take it all in. She was also worried about how Chris would take the news, especially as he was having to work during the day, visit Jane on his way home, then pick Kevin up and see to his needs. She was only too aware that he was tired and worried for her, and that he would have to carry the extra burden of telling the news to the rest of the family.

Jane told one of the nurses that she wanted a doctor to speak to Chris when he arrived to visit her. 'I felt news like that was best coming from a professional, who could explain all the dangers and reasons why the decision to abort had to be taken. He had to know everything that was going on, and I thought I'd miss out something important if I told him myself.'

When Chris arrived, Jane says that although he was shocked, he took the news calmly. 'We spent some time talking to the doctor,' she says. 'I was desperate to prevent an abortion. I told them I'd be willing to lie in bed for the rest of the pregnancy, but the doctor said I wouldn't live that long. My blood pressure was dangerously high. They said I already had a child who needed me. They said they didn't want to take my baby away, but there was no option, they had to save my life. So it was taken out of our hands.'

The results from Jane's blood tests were returned from Charing Cross Hospital the following day, confirming that she had a hydatidiform mole. The abortion was booked for Saturday morning, and although it was Jane's consultant's day off, he said he would come in especially to perform the operation.

On Friday night, the pastor from Jane's old church visited her. 'I was so amazed to see him. He said he'd felt he had to come and see me. He prayed for me, and read the passage from Romans 8:37–39, which ends, "Nothing shall separate us from the love of God." I felt so warm and peaceful.

'Then John arrived. He said he wanted to pray for the soul of the baby. I was really taken aback by that – I just couldn't take that on board. But he said, "It's your child, created and formed as a human being. Its life is going to be taken away from it because of this, and it needs to be released and given to God." I found it comforting, and when he prayed I felt a tremendous peace. And it was wonderful when he prayed the same scripture – "Nothing shall separate us from the love of God." '

Jane slept well and still felt at peace when she woke the next morning. But the operation was delayed because of an emergency, and she lay alone in her room, surrounded by screens, listening to the babies in the wards nearby. Fear and panic started to creep in as she lay there, but the nurses were 'fantastic, and kept coming in to hold my hand'.

After the operation, Jane was very ill. 'I had a drip in each arm, my blood pressure was taken every twenty minutes. Doctors kept being called because of the worry about the blood pressure. I kept being sick, and I had such a blinding headache, it felt as though my head was bleeding. I was delirious for hours – I don't remember Chris coming to see me, but Mum, who was sitting at my side all the time, says he did.

'I can remember being fed horrible soup, which I threw up straight away. And I can remember about 11 p.m. John came to sit with me, and he prayed. He said he'd come and give me communion the next day, which was Sunday.'

At six the next morning, a nurse brought Jane a cup of tea. And she was touched when the nurse, without being asked, washed the bedside table and laid a clean white cloth on it, in preparation for communion.

The simple communion was peaceful. But for the rest of the day Jane says she felt empty, in a vacuum. She found out afterwards that John had made enquiries about her the day before, and on finding out that she was seriously ill he had prayed in the Sunday morning service for angels to protect her. He also announced that all prospective visitors should go to Chris for permission to visit.

On Monday, Jane felt fit enough to walk alone to the bathroom. As she returned to her room, a new mother from the room next door spoke to her.

'What did you have – a boy or a girl?' she asked. Jane replied that there had been something wrong, and her baby had had to be taken away.

'She didn't know what to say,' Jane recalls. 'So I said to her, "What did you have? Can I see it?" I just knew I must go in and look at her baby. I stayed a few minutes, then went back to my room.

'When the doctor came in, I said I wanted to go home – I couldn't stay in the maternity wing any longer. He said if my blood pressure was stable I could go home the next day.'

Jane was discharged the following day, Tuesday, after two weeks in hospital. She was given drugs against infection, and told she must send monthly urine samples to Charing Cross Hospital for the next ten years. Bottles were posted monthly in a little box; Jane filled them and posted them back.

She also had to go to her own GP for monthly blood tests. Checks had to be made to ensure that cancerous tissue had not attached itself to the lining of the womb – and she was warned that if she conceived within the next two years, the pregnancy would have to be terminated.

'When I came home, I was in shock,' she says. 'My family and three close friends from church still carried on visiting, and helping with washing and meals. But I was alone on the third day out of hospital, when John came round, and I cried and cried. The hospital had warned me my hormonal imbalance meant my character might change, and I was as devastated by that as by losing the baby. I was so frightened I was going to change – I thought I was going to be horrible. John prayed for total healing, and that God would cast out fear.

'I felt very low for weeks. But in my daily readings, I kept reading about God caring for his children, about everyone being special. At the time, I was reading a book called *The good shepherd and his sheep*. It was mainly about a shepherd's experience with his sheep, and showing the parallel to Jesus the good shepherd (John 10). Over and over again, the message came across about how much the good shepherd loves, cares for and knows his sheep by name. Each one is special and precious. I thought, if God knows me so well, he knows about the loss.'

One reference in the book which really moved Jane was Psalm 139, a psalm of David the shepherd. 'For you created my inmost being – you knit me together in my mother's womb . . . My frame was not hidden from you, when I was made in the secret place . . . your eyes saw my unformed body' (vv 13 and 16).

'This child was created and formed, precious and known to God,' says Jane. 'Again the scripture from Romans 8 came back, for a third time: "Nothing shall separate us from the love of God." There is nothing – not even death can separate us. In the darkness I knew that God was there, and I had peace that I can only say came from him. In letting God come into my emotions, I received strength and hope to move on and receive God's healing touch. I still didn't know what it was all about, but I didn't question it after that.

'I never say I had an abortion. I didn't choose to have one. They terminated the pregnancy. It was taken away from me.'

Although Jane had been told she should not conceive for two years, she was given a clean bill of health after eighteen months, and was told it would be safe to have another child. Within three months, she found she was pregnant.

She was given special care and regular scans because of her recent history. When she was fifteen weeks, she had an internal examination and was told everything was fine. But she was also told that 'if anything happens', she should come straight to Casualty with her notes.

But at sixteen and a half weeks – the same time exactly as she had lost her second baby – Jane miscarried her third (and last) child.

Although she has no proof, Jane believes her cervix had been weakened by the suction abortion she'd had to undergo. An induced birth, with the worry about her blood pressure, had been considered too dangerous at the time. 'I think I'd been ripped apart,' she says.

It was just over two years after her last pregnancy had been terminated, and Jane was doing three early-morning stints each week, decorating cakes in a local bakery.

'When I arrived at work, my boss said I looked pale,' she remembers. 'I asked him to lift things for me, because I felt I shouldn't take any risks. A few minutes later I was standing up, piping a cake, when with no warning at all I saw a puddle all over the floor. And I realised it was coming from me.'

Jane recollects with horror that she walked up two flights of stairs to the toilet, where she found she was having a 'show'. She then walked back down the stairs and – remembering the doctor's instructions to bring her notes to Casualty – asked a shop assistant to take her home to collect the notes.

She arrived home at 8 a.m., went upstairs for the notes, and asked Chris to take Kevin to friends and then follow her to hospital. Back in the shop assistant's car, crawling through the rush hour traffic, she realised she was having contractions.

Eventually they arrived at Casualty, and Jane found herself alone in a cubicle, lying on the bed, bleeding heavily.

'A houseman examined me and said, "I'm afraid you're going to lose this baby." Then both he and another doctor said I was haemorrhaging so much that I could bleed to death. They gave me an injection to stop the bleeding, and then, to speed up the process, they terminated the pregnancy there and then. It was so painful, and a nurse had to hold me down while they did what they had to do. I often think of that nurse now – that poor lady, what she had to go through while she stood holding my shoulders.

'The baby was sloshing around in one of those cardboard sick-bowls,' Jane remembers. 'The doctors asked me if they could take the foetus away for examination, and I agreed, because I wanted to find out if it had the same thing wrong with it as the other baby. They didn't offer to let me see it – it probably wouldn't have been wise. It was still classed as a foetus, so that was the terminology they used. And I suppose they could also have used that word, rather than "baby", to make it less painful for me.

'By the time Chris got to Casualty, it was all over. The baby had been taken away. I was wheeled to the ward, and in the afternoon I was taken to theatre for a D&C operation. I was back home within two days. And that was that. There was nothing – no goodbyes, no funeral. I heard years later of a vicar who took memorial services for people who'd lost tiny babies and were unable to have funerals. I would have appreciated a service like that.'

After her first loss, Jane hadn't wanted to know the sex of her baby. But the second time, she found out the baby had been a girl. After she was discharged from hospital, her GP wanted to show her that this pregnancy hadn't been a repeat of the first. Trying to reassure her that the baby had been healthy, he handed her the report from the hospital to read for herself. 'But all I could see were the words "normal female foetus",' Jane recalls. 'They leapt out at me. It was so much harder knowing it was a girl. I felt an incredible sense of loss.

'In some ways, the second loss was more traumatic than the termination. The physical recovery was much quicker – I just had a few antibiotics. Friends and family supported me again. But I questioned it more the second time than the first. *Why* did it have to go wrong a second time?'

In the early weeks of the pregnancy, Jane had had anxiety attacks – what if she had another hydatidiform mole? But as the weeks went by and she remained healthy, the panic had subsided. She had started to tell people, and was receiving congratulations. 'We'd just told the Bible study group, and they'd prayed for the baby – and a few days later it had gone,' she recalls.

Then the 'if only' questions began. The most obvious – since she was standing up at work when the miscarriage began – was, 'If only I hadn't gone out to work, would it have been all right?' But during her first pregnancy she had worked full-time in the bakery until she was eight months, and nothing had gone wrong. It has taken years, she admits, for her to stop asking such questions. And some 'friends' added to the guilt, one saying, 'If you hadn't got up so early . . .' and another, 'You were working too much.'

'It's like that with bereavement,' says Jane. 'People either say nothing or feel they have to say something – and it's better if they don't.'

Other friends offered understanding and support. The staff from the bakery, devastated by what had happened – and on their premises, too – sent a bouquet of flowers. And one couple from church, whose baby was due at the same time as Jane's had been, realised what she must be feeling. Some months later they phoned to warn her that their baby was to be induced the next day. And as soon as their little girl was born, they phoned again, wanting her to hear the news from them straight away, not from anyone else.

Telling Kevin was another consideration which Jane hadn't had to cope with after the first loss. He was now four, old enough to know what was happening. He'd talked about the baby in mummy's tummy, and wondered whether he was going to have a brother or a sister.

'I had to tell him the baby had died and gone to be with Jesus, and he would look after it,' says Jane. 'He seemed to take it quite well at the time. Then, weeks later, he was playing with his friend Rebecca on the stairs. They were playing with dolls, putting them to bed. Suddenly I heard Kevin's voice, panic-stricken, crying, "Becca, Becca, my baby's dead!" Rebecca said, "Well, pray and ask Jesus to make it better." And Kevin replied, "But Jesus is going to look after it in heaven."

'I felt his response was healthy – he was acting out his loss in play, and at least he knew the baby was in heaven. But his anger came out much later, when a friend was pregnant and I said she could have my pram. Kevin said, "What are you doing with my baby's pram?" and I said I was giving it away. I hadn't thought it would affect him, but he was really angry. I sat down with him and talked about sharing, and reassured him we would get the pram back again.'

Jane found babies' baptisms in the Sunday services very traumatic. She cried through the first few she attended after the loss of her last baby. And at the first Christmas carol service she attended, the congregation began to sing 'Once in Royal David's City'. After the line, 'There his children gather round' she started to cry, and couldn't stop for the rest of the service. 'But you have to learn to cope with it,' she says. 'You have to go to baptisms, and even be a godparent.'

A close friend of Jane's, who had been infertile for years, eventually became pregnant and had a son. Jane felt very happy for her. But when she went to visit her friend in hospital, Jane found she was in the same room where Jane herself had spent two weeks when she had the termination. 'I couldn't believe it!' she says. 'I just thought, "You can't do this to me." But I went in, and I looked at the baby. He was beautiful, and I felt so happy – she'd waited ten years for a baby. But I just couldn't speak. All I could do was go out of the room and cry.'

Jane had always felt her experience wasn't as bad as that of parents who had had a healthy baby and then lost it. But years later, she was talking to a friend who had lost a baby at nine months old. 'I was saying it must have been so much harder for her than for me,' Jane recalls. 'After all, she'd got to know the baby, nursed it and played with it, so the pain must have been worse. But she said, "No, you're wrong, it's worse for you than it was for me. You never knew your baby; you were never able to care for it like I was." I thought it was incredibly generous of her to say that.'

Chris and Jane, frightened to go through the process of pregnancy and possible loss again, decided not to have another baby. Jane gave her maternity clothes to a friend – who gave them back after the birth of her baby. She then passed them on to another friend – and back they came again.

'The maternity clothes kept coming back,' says Jane. 'I started to feel annoyed. I kept giving them away, and people always felt they had to give them back. But why were they giving these things back to me – I didn't have any need of them. In 1993, when they were returned to me for the umpteenth time, I felt I couldn't cope with getting them back again, and I put them in the Third World clothes bin. I did it almost in annoyance, not grief. We were moving house at the time, and when I cleaned out the attic and found the high-chair still up there, I gave it to a neighbour.'

She has not found the experiences have turned her away from God, or made her doubt him. Neither does she remember being angry with God. 'I'm just not an angry person,' she says. 'I know everyone is supposed to have anger in them, and if they don't show it, it comes out in other ways. But if I *was* angry, I don't know what I did with it.

'I just felt, "I don't understand." And I don't think we ever understand why.' After her first loss particularly, she recalls the tremendous sense of peace, a knowledge that even though she didn't understand it, God was in it.

'You always remember; the sense of loss never goes away. But you do feel for other people in a similar situation. I've prayed that

God would use the pain and the whole experience to his glory. God can take that pain if you offer it to him, and he can use it so that some good will come out of it.'

And in her counselling ministry at her local church, Jane has been able to see good coming out of her pain, as she identifies with and cries with grieving people. 'Maybe that's where the anger's gone – it's been channelled into praying with other people,' she says.

'I know God's sustained me,' Jane concludes. 'People have always said I'm so calm and "together", when I should be in a heap. Even as a child, I went through some awful things, but I cried out to God. And he's helped me ever since.'

7

Lydia Dawn: our missing child

Karen miscarried her first child at three months in 1978. She and Andy had been married for three years, and both of them were shocked by what had happened. 'It was totally unexpected,' says Karen. 'We thought people got pregnant, and nine months later they had a baby. Nobody told us things could go wrong.'

Although they were upset, Karen says they were occupied with work, and assumed that a normal pregnancy would follow. And when she became pregnant three months later, she did indeed have a normal pregnancy. Their 9lb daughter Naomi was born safely in 1979.

But eighteen months later, Karen suffered another miscarriage, this time at ten weeks. She can't remember that the loss hurt too much, and in fact her main emotion was relief. Looking back, she realised that she'd felt pressurised to get pregnant, because all her friends were. The 'two-year gap' between children seemed to be the expected thing.

'The baby was due in Christmas week 1980, and I felt panicky about it,' says Karen. 'I discovered I didn't want two children under the age of two. I'd planned the baby.'

The couple were advised by their GP to wait three months before starting another baby. And during that time, they decided after all that they wanted another child as soon as possible. Karen went back to the doctor to ask if there was anything that could be done to stop another baby miscarrying. The doctor agreed that she should have hormonal help, and told her that next time she became pregnant she should take hormone tablets each day.

At the end of the three months, Karen became pregnant straight away. Apart from being terribly sick, as she had been when she was expecting Naomi, there were no complications. She felt the sickness was a positive sign that all was well – when she was pregnant with the two babies that miscarried, she hadn't felt sick at all. She had the hormone tablets, and when the pregnancy continued beyond the three-month stage both Karen and Andy felt a sense of relief.

But when she was about eighteen weeks pregnant, Karen again started to be concerned. She knew two other women who were expecting their babies in the same week as hers, and they had felt their babies move. Karen felt no movement. In the weeks following, Karen did feel a little movement from her baby – but by that stage her friends' babies were moving quickly and frequently.

She kept telling the midwives of her concern, but she was told she was suffering with nerves because of the previous miscarriages.

At her twenty-four week ante-natal appointment, Karen's doctor seemed to spend a long time pushing on her abdomen, feeling the shape of the baby. Then, without explaining why, he told her he was booking her in for a scan.

It wasn't until weeks later, at her post-natal appointment, that she was told why the doctor had sent her for a scan. He had felt a large lump at the back of the baby's neck, which he suspected to be severe spina bifida.

Andy went with Karen for the scan, and as there was no one to look after two-year-old Naomi, she had to go too. Karen remembers that the radiographer seemed embarrassed and rather upset. He asked her if she was in any pain, and she told him she wasn't. Again, it wasn't until her post-natal appointment that Karen found out why the radiographer was upset. Looking at the screen, he could clearly see a baby with severe spina bifida.

Karen was also studying the screen, and she too saw that something wasn't right. 'There was a round thing which appeared to be attached to the baby,' she says. 'I asked what it was, and I was told I seemed to have cysts. But I could see it was attached to the baby, not to me.'

The scan was not clear, the radiographer told her, so he couldn't be sure about the cysts. He told Karen and Andy to go to another hospital, where the ultrasound machine was more modern, for a second scan.

Karen doesn't remember any of the bus journey home. 'I was scared out of my mind,' she says. 'The ultrasound showed there was a heartbeat, so all we knew for sure was that the baby was alive. It was obvious there was something seriously wrong, but nobody would tell us. I was totally panic-stricken. All I could say was, "It's going to die." Andy kept calm for me, telling me everything would be all right. And all this was happening in the company of a lively two-year-old.'

They had over a week to wait for the second scan. Both of them spent the time in a daze. Andy found he was still burying his fears and feelings in order to stay strong for Karen. He tried to stop her worrying. And his mother kept phoning, also worrying, and both Andy and Karen were put in the position of having to reassure *her*.

The second scan, when Karen was twenty-six weeks pregnant, showed that the baby had no heartbeat. But the two radiographers who were present were even then unable to tell her the truth. One said the baby must be asleep. 'Even *I* knew that if there's no heartbeat, it means the baby's dead!' says Karen.

The other commented, 'You're still young.' 'And what does *that* mean, except that this baby's dead, and you're young enough to have another one?' asks Karen. It seemed the radiographers still couldn't say anything, and they merely asked Karen and Andy to return the next day to speak to the consultant.

Karen says she totally blanked out. She remembers nothing of the twenty-four hours between one appointment and the next. When they went to see the consultant, they were told that the baby was dead. He told them to go home and 'let things take their course'. Karen would go into labour within the next fifteen days, he said.

So they went home. Karen went to bed, and stayed there for a few days. They avoided people. Everyone still thought she was pregnant – what could she say if she met anyone? On their sixth wedding anniversary, they went to Brighton for the day. They could be anonymous there, where no one knew them.

They decided not to tell anyone except three couples who were close friends from church. Then one day their vicar rang the doorbell.

'He just arrived on the doorstep – one of our friends must have told him what had happened,' says Andy. 'And he was fantastic. He wasn't afraid to talk about it. I thought he might be nervous or embarrassed – but then I suppose he was used to life and death. He was sympathetic and practically helpful. He was the one who suggested a funeral.'

'Inside, I'd wanted to have a funeral, but I hadn't said so,' says Karen. 'I wasn't quite twenty-eight weeks pregnant, and at that time babies weren't considered viable before then, so there's not normally a funeral. And it meant that we still couldn't bury the baby in consecrated ground.'

'We wondered how we were going to pay for the funeral,' says Andy. 'We hadn't got any money. And our vicar said, "Don't worry, we'll pay." He got things organised, and made an appointment for me to see the funeral director. I was totally naïve – I'd no idea really. The funeral director asked questions and explained or suggested things. It was the first funeral I'd ever been to, and Karen had only been to one.'

'Andy dealt with it all,' says Karen. 'I couldn't have planned it. The only thing the vicar said I had to make sure of was that the hospital didn't dispose of the body.'

One morning, after a week of hiding from people, Karen rang her GP. 'There I was, looking pregnant, but the baby was dead, and I wanted it to go,' she says. 'I didn't feel a horror of the baby because it was dead. That wasn't the awful thing. But I just wanted it to end.

'The thing that was bothering me most was that it was coming up to Mothering Sunday, and I didn't want to go into labour on that day. It would be too ironic. So I asked if my GP could arrange for the baby to be born before Mothering Sunday, which was in two days time.'

The doctor agreed that she should be induced, and arranged for her to go into hospital that same afternoon. But by the evening she was still waiting. The consultant, standing by Karen's bedside, told her he couldn't induce her because 'there were other people waiting to have *live* babies.'

'I found him callous and unpleasant,' she says. 'He'd been insensitive at the first appointment, when he'd told us the baby was dead. Now he was dismissing our baby because it wasn't "live". And the next day, he was even worse.'

The next day, Saturday, Karen was still waiting to be induced. That evening, the consultant brought consent forms for her to sign. But they were abortion consent forms.

'The nurse told him they were the wrong forms,' says Karen. 'But he actually said that it didn't matter. I did sign them, because I knew the baby was dead, so I knew an abortion wouldn't hurt it. But I was upset, because although it wouldn't hurt, it would damage the baby's body.'

Karen had been kept waiting too long. She went into labour naturally on the Sunday morning – Mothering Sunday, 29 March 1981. Even though it was the day she'd dreaded giving birth, she was still glad she'd gone into labour naturally, and hadn't had to go through with an abortion.

'The labour lasted four hours, and I was on my own – Andy had to look after Naomi,' says Karen. 'The nurses came in from time to time. Every time the midwife came in, I kept saying, "You've got to keep the body, we've got to have a funeral." It was the day of the first London Marathon, and I kept hearing Marathon reports. I wondered who would win, but in the end they beat me.

'The labour wasn't too difficult, except that it was difficult to push the baby out at the end, because of the misshapen part of the neck – although I didn't know about that at the time.'

Karen had been told previously by her health visitor that the baby would be flaky and decomposed, and she had been strongly advised not to look at it. But when the midwife let Karen look at her daughter, although she looked blue she was otherwise a normal baby.

'The midwife wrapped her in a blanket, which covered the back of her neck. Looking back on it, I realise she was holding her in such a way that I wouldn't see she was damaged.

'I loved her. I still bonded with her despite the fact she was dead. She was still my baby, and I wanted her. She was pretty.

The midwife showed her to me briefly, then I let her go. The midwife seemed embarrassed and that made me embarrassed, too. I just looked at her before they took her away. But if I'd been left alone, I'd have picked her up.'

When Andy arrived a short time later, it was assumed he wouldn't want to look at the baby. And it didn't occur to him to ask to see her. Andy brought Naomi, and Karen remembers the atmosphere being 'very strained'.

'I remember thinking what funny clothes he'd dressed Naomi in,' she says. Andy describes the scene as 'pretty peculiar. I didn't know what to think. We'd had a week to get used to the fact that she was dead, so part of me was relieved that it was over.'

Karen came out of hospital the next day. And five days after the birth, the funeral service was held for Lydia Dawn at the crematorium. Karen and Andy had chosen the name before their baby was born. They had no special requests for the service, and all Karen remembers about it is that 'a Sunday-school-type hymn was played'. Some people from their church were there, but no one from either of their families attended.

'We weren't close to our families then,' says Karen. 'Lydia just wasn't mentioned. I felt angry and upset, and I longed for them to talk about it. I wanted to say to Andy's mum, "She was your grandchild." It was as if nothing had happened.'

A week later, when Karen and Andy went back to the crematorium for the ashes, Karen was taken aback. They were handed something that looked like an ice-cream carton, and she couldn't believe a tiny baby could produce so many ashes. They took the ashes to a playground in a nearby park. 'Naomi played there,' says Karen, 'and we would have taken Lydia there too. So the logic was that we took her there anyway.'

The three couples from church who had been told about the baby gave their time. 'They were on hand, and very helpful practically, with cooking and babysitting,' says Karen. One day Karen felt agoraphobic – she couldn't get out of the house, and she needed to do some shopping. She rang one of the friends, who came straight round and went shopping with her. 'Even if I sounded daft, she still went with me,' says Karen.

Another of the friends invited Andy, Karen and Naomi for Sunday dinners. And three months later, that same friend looked after Naomi for a week so Andy and Karen could have a holiday alone. She, too, had lost a baby a few years before, and was aware of what the couple were going through. No one else in the church offered help, but Karen says the congregation knew that they were being supported by the three couples, so let them get on with it. She found the care of the vicar and the three couples was quite enough.

They didn't get any cards from friends, and only a few from acquaintances. But Karen says they all seemed to treat it lightly. Some people wrote, 'I hope you get over your miscarriage.' Others sent 'get well soon' messages. 'I wasn't ill!' says Karen. 'This was negating my baby. What I really wanted were congratulations cards – I'd had a baby, after all. So I asked Andy to buy me a ring, as a gift for having Lydia. I wore it as long as the pain lasted.'

At the post-natal check, which was after the baby's autopsy, Karen was at last told about the spina bifida. She knew that photographs had been taken of the scan and asked if she could see them, but the doctor said there weren't any. Karen saw him slipping something into the back of the file and knew he was lying.

She had nothing at all to remind her of Lydia. It wasn't until four years later, when she had changed her doctor, that she again brought up the subject of the scan photographs. The new GP gave them to her.

In the weeks after Lydia's death, several people told Karen and Andy, 'You're managing really well!' They both felt that meant they'd *got* to manage. 'But I didn't want to manage, I wanted to shout and scream!' says Karen.

Andy went back to work and, so far as Karen could see, got on with his normal life. 'I just *had* to get on and work,' says Andy. 'My colleagues didn't talk about what had happened, although they knew about it. I suppose I was glad to go, to get into another world. I probably buried my grief in work. I suppose I've never grieved properly. I feel I should do, even now, to get things out of the way – both for Lydia and for my parents, whose deaths I've not worked through either. I find it difficult to let feelings go and grieve properly. I know it's not good. It all creeps up on me and reminds me now and again, and then it hurts. Looking back, I can see I didn't handle it at all well.'

'I resented the fact that Andy could go out and get into another world,' says Karen. 'I had to stay at home and cope. I got angry with Andy about that. And I also got angry with God. One day, when I was feeling particularly bad, I told God he was a male chauvinist pig, because Andy was going to work and I was at home. But God reminded me about what had happened to his son, and that stopped me in my tracks.'

Because Andy found it difficult to express his feelings, Karen often felt frustrated. 'I'd tell him how I felt about something,' she says, 'and then ask him how he felt about it. And I'd get silence. I felt angry because he wasn't expressing things. He'd say he understood how I felt, and I thought, "If you understand it, why aren't you responding more to it?" '

But she tries to understand and analyse why Andy didn't respond more. 'I suppose I was expressing my feelings, and maybe he felt he had no room to express his. And he comes from a family like that, too. And women are expected to grieve more than men, so I had more licence to grieve openly. Andy says I could never be accused of burying my emotions.

'I don't think it pulled us apart, though. It didn't bring us together, either – it was just "happening". It could easily have pulled us apart, but the time of anger and resentment only lasted a few weeks. I knew I had to put my life together. My anger ended when I told God what I thought of him.'

'I went through phases of blaming God and being angry with him,' says Andy. 'And of asking, "What did we do wrong, there must be something?" I eventually concluded it hadn't happened because of anything we'd done – although even now the thought still pops up occasionally. But it had no long-term effect on my faith, just a "wobble" that didn't last very long. Neither of us ever stopped believing in God, or in Christ dying for us.'

Although Karen's anger only lasted a few weeks, she says she was still left with 'a great, aching hole'.

'I cried a lot,' she says. 'I wasn't grieving for a person I'd known, but for my plans and hopes and dreams. I'd already planned what I'd get the baby for Christmas; I'd looked in Mothercare and seen matching clothes for three-year-olds and babies. And I'd feel very frustrated with Naomi. She's strong-willed, and every time she did something awful, I'd think, "I bet your sister wouldn't have done that." She probably would have – it was just a fantasy.'

At the mother and toddler group where Karen took Naomi, a woman she hardly knew approached her. She had lost a child in a cot death, and had several other children. 'She gave me no platitudes,' says Karen. 'She just came up and said, "You can't replace her, but it will get better." I felt there was hope there. She was the only one who said anything like that, and it was the most helpful thing that was said to me. Other people seemed to assume that because I'd already got one child, losing one is easier. And they'd see the next as a replacement. But it's not like that. All children are individuals.'

As the mother at the toddler group had told her, the intense pain did start to get better. 'It sort of gradually faded,' says Karen. 'There were low spots when Lydia would have been due, and there were waves of grief, with some days being bad and others not so bad.'

The couple's GP suggested they went for genetic counselling, and made them an appointment at Guy's Hospital. No one knew the cause of Karen's two earlier miscarriages, but they were told that if those pregnancies had been spina bifida babies, there was a one in ten chance that another child would also be spina bifida. If those babies were not, then there was a one in twenty chance that the next child would be. Karen also asked what chance Naomi had of carrying a spina bifida baby in the future, and was told it would be one in four hundred.

They were told about a new research programme, which hoped to show that folic acid could prevent spina bifida. Karen felt if she went through with that programme, even if it didn't work for her, it could make Lydia's life meaningful and significant for others.

Even with this reassurance, Andy and Karen didn't want to rush into another pregnancy. 'Three out of four not working out was a high proportion,' says Karen. 'We both wanted to go ahead, but we were scared.'

They discussed adoption, but decided against it. Eventually, they decided to try for another baby of their own, and Karen became pregnant nine months after Lydia's death.

She took vitamin B and folic acid from the time they started trying for a baby, until thirteen weeks into the pregnancy. She experienced no side-effects, and the pregnancy continued without any problems. Karen was frightened when the baby didn't move for any length of time, and found she had to have Andy with her for all the scans – her past experience had made her terrified of them.

Asa was born on 1 October 1982. 'His name means "God heals",' says Karen. 'And a lot of healing happened with Asa. He wasn't a replacement, but the end of a chapter and the beginning of the next chapter. The pain became less acute. Life assumed normality.'

Three years later, Andy and Karen had another daughter, Susannah.

'For a long time I didn't know how to count my children,' says Karen. 'Had I three? For a long time after Susannah was born, I said I had four children. But then I thought it was confusing for other people. And should it have been six? Now I think of Lydia as our "missing child".

'We always wanted three children,' Karen continues. 'One day, Susannah said to me, "You wanted three children, so I wouldn't have been born if Lydia hadn't died." It was really hard – because she was right. So I said, "Yes, but you are here and your sister isn't, and we chose to have you, and we love you very much."'

Andy says Asa also questions it occasionally. 'They have a curiosity,' he says. 'And it's never been a secret.'

Naomi has told Karen that she feels guilty and upset because she can't remember anything about Lydia, or about what happened when she was two years old. Karen says she asks questions, such as 'Was I there at the funeral?'

'She certainly had a rough pre-school time,' says Karen. 'I was either stressed or grieving, and I kept saying I was tired, or sick, or I couldn't pick her up. But no one can say for sure what effect it's had on her. I used to feel guilty about it, but then I realised I didn't bring about those circumstances; it wasn't anything I did.'

Karen says the whole experience took the ground from under her. 'I used to plan ahead,' she says. 'I thought you could map your life out. Now I know I can't rely on my plans; I must live from day to day. I don't panic like I used to, and I work round things. It's changed me like that. And it's made me more sensitive – I still weep buckets if I hear about a child being hurt.

'I went to a support group for a while, but in the end I felt that I was just opening up the scars. I'd got to get on with life. And for a couple of years, if I wanted to think or pray, I'd go to "Lydia's spot" – the playground where we'd sprinkled her ashes. But it became less and less frequent. I thought, "Why am I doing this? She's not here. What am I going back for?"

'I wore the ring Andy bought me for six or seven years, and the grief faded and faded. One day, during a church service, I felt God was saying to me, "What are you hanging on to? Take the ring off." So I did. And these days, I just wear it now and again, not for sentimental reasons, but because it looks nice.

'But that doesn't mean I've deliberately buried Lydia, just that I've not deliberately hung on to her. She's behind us now; she's not an ongoing person. We don't build our lives on the fact that it's happened. So even if we had pictures of her, we wouldn't have them on display.

'Life can return to normal, even when your baby's died. You don't keep them alive, because they're not. Does that sound hard? You can continue, and go forward. You don't forget the baby, but you don't have to keep going back – not unless it helps somebody else.'

8

Longed-for child

When Simon and Pauline were married in May 1976, they were both keen to have children. So when they discovered Pauline was pregnant in early 1978, they were thrilled.

Pauline had a difficult pregnancy. She was sick for the first sixteen weeks, and kept experiencing small bleeds. From four months onwards she had 'practice' contractions. Her GP and the hospital reassured her that it was nothing to worry about, and she was told to be 'philosophical' about it. But it turned out to be a warning: Pauline had a weak cervix.

At 10 a.m. on 14 July, when she was twenty-eight weeks pregnant, Pauline's waters broke. She didn't panic; she says she had 'no real problems' about having a premature baby. She had qualified as a midwife at a top premature baby unit where they were pioneers in neonatal care, and in all her time there she had never seen a baby die.

Unfortunately, the premature unit where Pauline's own baby was to spend her short life was not that same one.

Simon describes the labour as 'botched'. When they arrived at the hospital at midday, the staff attempted to stop the labour with an intravenous infusion, although Pauline says it was obvious it wasn't going to stop.

'Then I was delivered by a midwife, when it should have been a doctor doing a forceps delivery to protect the baby's delicate head,' says Pauline. 'I can remember trying to hang on to wait for the doctor and the paediatrician, who I felt should have both been present at the birth. The episiotomy was done with blunt scissors, after they'd searched for some sharp ones and couldn't find any.'

But Laura Naomi was born safely at 4.46 a.m. on 15 July, at twenty-eight weeks six days gestation, and weighing only 2lb 11½oz. Her Apgar score was good, she cried well, and didn't need any help with her breathing or any oxygen. So although she was whisked away before Pauline could see her, Pauline says she still wasn't unduly worried.

On the second day, Laura stopped breathing for a few seconds. But even though she went on to have more of these apnoea attacks, Pauline still felt confident – she knew this was something that could happen to premature babies. Laura survived the attacks and even started to gain weight. A week after the birth she began to stop breathing again, and 'gave cause for concern'. Again, she survived that setback, and the hospital staff told Pauline and Simon they were 'home and dry'.

Pauline had been discharged from hospital, but visited Laura twice a day. In the morning her mother accompanied her, and in the evening she went with Simon, after he had finished his job as a computer scientist. They had no car, so relied on friends from church to give them lifts.

On the twelfth day, the hospital staff told Pauline and Simon that Laura was 'ill'. They went to the hospital in the afternoon, and sat with Laura throughout her crisis in the evening. But by 11 p.m. she appeared to have stabilised, and the staff advised them to go home and get some rest.

'I don't know to this day why we went home,' says Pauline. 'Did we expect to see her in the morning?' Half an hour after they arrived home, the hospital rang to say Laura had died at 11.45 p.m.

They were told not to go back to the hospital that night, but to stay at home. 'We were so young and shocked that we never challenged it,' says Pauline. Her diary entry for that day, 27 July 1978, reads: 'Laura Naomi died age twelve and a half days old. Loved by us but chosen by God.'

The next day, when they went to the unit to collect the death certificate, they saw the empty incubator. 'It really hit home then,' says Pauline. The death certificate recorded the first cause of death as 'prematurity' and the second as 'pneumonia'. Pauline says the hospital had been trying to feed Laura too much, and the milk had overflowed into her lungs, causing the pneumonia.

'I never thought she'd die,' says Pauline. 'When she'd survived the first three days, we were told there was a good chance everything would be all right. And after she'd passed the first week they said we were home and dry. And then she died at twelve days.'

Simon and Pauline's GP told them afterwards that half the babies who died in that hospital needn't have died there. 'She didn't say, "They didn't take enough care", but that was the upshot of it,' says Pauline. 'There weren't enough trained people there who knew what they were doing. That was the hardest thing to cope with.'

The day before the labour started, Simon and Pauline had been shopping to buy baby things. 'We'd spent two hundred pounds on clothes, a cot, sheets, towels, nappies, blankets and the baby bath,' says Pauline. 'It was all still in the lounge when I went into hospital. After Laura died I wanted to put everything away myself. I didn't want anyone else to do it for me because it would suggest we'd never had her. I'd planned so much for the birth – and it was all planning into nothingness.' The only time either of them had touched their daughter was when they had put a finger through the hole in the incubator.

Nobody gave the couple any advice on how to deal with their feelings, or what practical arrangements needed to be made after a death. Left to themselves, they arranged for a funeral to be held at the crematorium. But they felt unable to attend.

'We wouldn't have been able to cope with seeing such a small coffin,' says Pauline. 'Yet at the same time we were torn, because we felt we were neglecting and deserting Laura. But our minister went in our place to make sure it was done properly. Then three days later we had a small family service at the crematorium, attended just by us, our parents and our minister. We'd already been up to the garden of remembrance and chosen a spot to sprinkle her ashes. It was at the edge of the garden where there was a dovecote and rabbits running through the ferns. We felt it was a place she would have liked.

'We had no regrets about not attending the funeral,' Pauline continues. 'Although, looking back now, perhaps we should have had a funeral service, not for our sake but for those friends who had never seen Laura and so afterwards found it hard to deal with our grief. Perhaps they would have been more supportive if we'd had a service.'

People from the church had given them lifts to the hospital while Laura was alive, and had paid for the funeral. 'While they could do something positive like that, they were great,' says Pauline. 'They'd all been praying, and had felt sure that God was going to heal Laura. But as soon as she died they didn't know what to say, and so they avoided us. They couldn't cope with the intensity of our feelings. That was almost as big a hurt as losing Laura.'

Simon and Pauline felt alone and isolated – a feeling compounded by the fact that their parents didn't know how to support them either. Pauline says it was a new situation for them as well, and they just didn't know how to respond. At lunch, before the family service at the crematorium, Pauline's father had turned to Simon's father and asked, 'How are your geraniums?'

The weekend after the funeral, thinking it would help to get away from home, they went to stay for a week in Wales with an old nursing colleague of Pauline's and her husband.

'They did care for us,' says Pauline. 'But then they ruined it when Peter questioned us about our "spiritual state", and wanted to pray with us. We couldn't handle that. We told him we had just lost our daughter and weren't in any condition to think about our spiritual state! I told him that at that moment, I hated God.

'Now, I'd advise anyone not to go away too soon after the death, even though you feel you want to,' she adds.

After they returned home, the couple's minister started a series of visits. 'He'd just sit there not saying anything,' says Pauline. 'One day, he sat in silence for thirty minutes, then as he got up to go, he asked how we were. I hit the roof!

'The next day he sent a letter addressed to just me, quoting some phrases of how others had been through trials as well. A couple of weeks later he lent me a book by one of the old hymn-writers, and on the very first page I read the words, "Because of the sins of the mother, the child died." We couldn't believe such insensitivity. We returned the book to him, and asked him not to call any more.'

Pauline says she found it very hard to talk to God during the months after Laura's death. 'My policy was very much, "You got me into this, so you get me out of it," ' she recalls.

'I felt incredibly angry with God. Looking back now, I realise there's nothing wrong with that. He's certainly big enough to take it. Jesus himself felt lonely and deserted on the cross, even though by faith he knew God was there. If he could feel neglected, then surely a mere child like me could feel the same? I knew by faith that God was there, even though it didn't feel like it.

'But other Christians found our being honest with God hard to handle. They were advising us to get back into homegroups – they didn't realise we needed time out. They seemed to think we had a spiritual problem because we couldn't join in normal church life straight away. They told us to "praise the Lord anyway" and get on with life, so God could reward us. But it didn't seem right to pray and do all the "right things" to get the result we wanted. That's like putting your money in a slot machine and getting out what you want. I wanted to look at everything blackly, so then anything else could only be better.'

She found the comments of other people one of the worst things to deal with. Two weeks after the funeral, a friend of many years' standing wrote a letter asking if they were feeling better and announcing she was pregnant. Another member of the church, on being introduced to Pauline, said, 'Ah yes, it's Pauline who lost the baby.' There were others who made what she describes as 'silly' comments, such as 'You're young yet' and 'You can always have another one.' One comment that particularly upset them was 'Everything will be fine, this time next year you'll have a baby.' 'How can people say that?' asks Pauline. 'They can't know; they can't be sure.'

Pauline was desperate for space to talk through her feelings – yet she was unable to do that without being made to feel she was in the wrong. Six weeks after Laura's death, feeling very depressed, she wrote in her diary, 'Why can't people understand? Why can't they even try?'

Almost immediately after Pauline wrote that diary entry, several things happened. The son of one of the church members, who had lost a baby himself, wrote to reassure them that their feelings were normal and honest, and they weren't going mad. The letter was 'a ray of light' to Pauline. Suddenly there was someone who understood how they felt. She had indeed begun to feel she was going mad and that her feelings were wrong. The couple went to stay with these new friends for a weekend, and spent much time talking.

Then another letter arrived, this time from a fourteen-year-old girl, who wrote that she was very sorry about what had happened to the baby, that she couldn't understand because she had never had children herself, but she was praying for them. Pauline started to realise that some people 'out there' did care. Her comment in her diary was that this girl had conquered fear more easily than many older Christians.

At about the same time, an old friend told Pauline to 'tell God exactly how you feel', because he would understand. She found it so helpful to hear those simple words. Until that point, all she had heard was people telling her what she should do and say, how she should behave and how she ought to feel. Now, she felt as if she had been given permission to grieve.

Again, at that time, Pauline contacted the Compassionate Friends, an organisation of bereaved parents supporting one another. She found it a great help to talk to other parents who knew what she was going through. Although they never met, they spoke on the phone and wrote to each other. Two other women in particular, one who had lost a four-year-old child, and the other a five-day-old baby, became her regular correspondents. Through their letters, Pauline says they were able to express their feelings of loss, and to work through the more bizarre feelings they shared, knowing the other person would understand. She found it healing to write everything down, and to realise her feelings weren't abnormal.

Pauline had written a poem soon after Laura's death, and it was included in the Compassionate Friends' magazine.

My arms reach out to hold the child I never held,
My breasts weep for the child they never suckled,
My lips tingle to kiss the child I never kissed,
My fingers stir to caress her face as they did just once before,
My heart yearns to give that child the love she hardly had,
And my soul grieves for my child, the child that I bore,
My flesh, our flesh,
Oh Lord, why did you need her so?
Why take her when she knew no life?
We would have loved her, we would have cared,
But you did not give us a chance.

My child, grieve not the child you lost,
She's safe in the arms of Jesus,
She's clutched to the breast of the loving one,
His lips kiss to wipe away your tears,
His fingers trace her smile, safe with her Lord,
His heart overflows with more love than you can ever give,
His soul is one with hers.
My child, she is safe, she's perfect,
I've kept her from all the sin of your world,
She's too precious to me, to live that life
Where greed and lust and grief abound.
She is your child, but she's my child too.
I lent her to you for just a short while.
Do not fear, my child, I have a plan,
Do not try to understand.

But, Lord, she is my child.
Will I never have a child to hold and love?
Oh sinful world, why is it so, why could you not obey?
Accept the Christ, he died for you.

Perhaps then I could have my child.
Where are you, Lord? The way is so dark,
Why can't I understand?
What future have you got for me?
Why can't I understand?

The new friendships helped Pauline – but she still felt terribly depressed. Reading through her diary now, she can remember how desperate she was to find peace, to find meaning to the hurt and pain, and to be able to see God's hand in it all. Sometimes she ran out of words to express what she was feeling.

'It felt as if we were living in a nightmare,' she says. 'I was grieving so much that at times I forgot who I was grieving for. We had no real memories of Laura. We had never held her, and we didn't really know her. The memories we did have were all filled with pain. The physical pain of her birth, the emotional pain of watching a tiny child fighting for her life, and the overwhelming pain of her dying. The anguish of having nothing to show for it except a few blurred photographs. You feel you're grieving the pain, rather than Laura herself.'

'There isn't a person to grieve for,' says Simon. 'The hospital staff said, "Remember her as she was" – but that's difficult if you have no memories. There's nothing of Laura that you can tell other people about. She had no personality. It's not her you talk about – she's almost incidental. You talk about the birth, the pain surrounding it, but not Laura. As the years go on, you wonder what you're grieving for. It just becomes an event, and you feel guilty because you can't feel anything. You try to find things to latch on to, so you latch on to the pain that other people caused you.'

'We were told by one person that it must be easier to lose a baby than an older child, because you've got to know the older child,' Simon continues. 'But part of our pain is exactly that – we didn't know our child. And then because other people didn't know her either, it was hard for them to equate her death with so much pain, so they had the "you can replace her" attitude.'

Simon found it hard to cope with Pauline's grief and depression as well as his own. 'Our grief came out in different ways,' he says.

'I was confused. Intellectually I could work through some of it, although I was always wondering why it happened. And there was some resentment. But there was a difference in our feelings. For a father, the bonding occurs after the birth, but for a mother it's there at the beginning. My emotions were split between grief for Laura and concern for Pauline. The worst thing was not knowing what I could do to help Pauline. There were emotions in her that I'd never come across before – and that I was surprised by. I could understand her grief, but there was nothing at all that I could say to her. I couldn't experience her feelings, I could only love her, and listen, and hold her. It did bring us closer.'

'Simon was able to get on with life,' says Pauline. 'He had his work to occupy him, whereas I had nothing. He tried very hard to understand. I desperately wanted his support, yet at the same time I found it hard to accept, as I doubted that he missed Laura as much as I did. I found it hard to appreciate that he couldn't feel Laura's death as much as me. But then I had already bonded with her while I was carrying her.'

'We learned to rely on each other, and we learned not to trust other people,' she says. But Simon adds, 'The problem with that is that it cuts other people off.'

Six months after Laura died, Simon and Pauline decided to leave their church. 'I was desperately crying out for help and support, and I didn't feel I was getting any,' says Pauline. 'Looking back, I realise there were two couples who were prepared to befriend us. They did come round, and they let me talk, but they weren't able to really understand what we were going through. But there were people who'd say they'd come round, and I'd rely on them and wait for them, and they didn't turn up. Others would say "How are you?" but wouldn't really want to know. And a few crossed the road to avoid us, as if we had the plague. Even the minister couldn't cope with us. We felt let down by people; we weren't getting anywhere. We could be anonymous in a different church, and that helped. It was a good move.'

Four months after their church move, Pauline found she was pregnant again. Her feelings were confused. She wanted the child she was expecting – but she wanted the child she had lost. She wanted Laura, not just 'a baby'. And she was angry that she had to go through a pregnancy again. These mixed emotions increased her guilt.

Writing to the two mothers from the Compassionate Friends became particularly important at this time. All three had become pregnant at the same time, and again they all found they were experiencing the same emotions. They had shared, too, the emotional difficulties of conceiving another child. Wanting a baby so much, sex had become something that happened to try and become pregnant. 'It was a means to an end,' says Pauline. 'We kept temperature charts to find the most fertile time of the month, and the sex was just a ritual, not purely an act of love.'

Throughout the pregnancy, Pauline feared that what had happened with Laura could happen again. At least this time the weak cervix had been noted. She was transferred to a different hospital, and received special treatment. At twenty-eight weeks, she was admitted for a month's rest.

Simon and Pauline's second daughter was born one month early. It was New Year's Day 1980, eighteen months after Laura's birth. After a very long labour, the baby was born by epidural Caesarean. 'I remember the delivery as funny,' says Pauline. 'It was so outrageous. The registrar had been at an all-night New Year's Eve party, and he came down to theatre still wearing his party hat. And I wasn't at all worried.'

They called their daughter Mara, which means 'bitter', and some people thought that was the reason Simon and Pauline chose the name. In fact they chose it for two very different reasons. First, the root name for Mara is 'Mary', which means 'longed-for child'.

Also, they wanted a name for their second child which would link in with Laura's name. In the Old Testament book of Ruth, when Naomi and Ruth returned to Bethlehem, Naomi told the women of the town, 'Do not call me Naomi, call me Mara.' Laura's second name was Naomi, and Pauline's second name is Ruth.

'I was so pleased to have Mara, but still Laura held my first feelings,' says Pauline. 'My parents always referred to Mara as their first grandchild. But she wasn't, she was their second. Laura wasn't acknowledged at all. Our relationship with my parents dropped off from the time Laura died.

'We were delighted with Mara. We couldn't believe that we had our much-wanted child. There was real rejoicing that our love had produced our own child; the wonder of God's creation astounded us. She was such a happy, contented baby, and we were amazed that we could love anyone as much as we did her. She was a pleasure to be with, and we enjoyed watching her grow and develop over the months.'

When Mara was about twenty months old, the couple started thinking about having another baby. They didn't want to have too long a gap between the children, but at the same time were reluctant to go ahead with trying because they were enjoying Mara so much and couldn't believe that they could love another child as much as they loved her.

However, when Mara was nearly three, Thomas was born, and Simon and Pauline found they were able to love another child as much as they loved Mara. Again Pauline had a difficult pregnancy, and Thomas was born two weeks early, in a planned Caesarean delivery.

'Time doesn't heal,' says Simon. 'When Mara was born, there wasn't a sudden break in our grief. It was a moving through. Time helps you adjust to it and live with it, but it certainly doesn't heal. It's always there.'

'In time we began to think that God considered us to be special people because he had chosen our daughter to be with him,' says Pauline. 'We began to feel privileged because God had chosen her. At the same time we wondered why God had chosen Laura, and not Mara or Thomas. Surely if to be with God is our hope, then he should have taken all of them – but no way did I want him to! Our thoughts were certainly confused!'

Even before they were married, Simon and Pauline had planned to foster children. Now that they felt their own natural family was complete, they started to discuss the possibility again. But there was a difference. This time, they were talking about fostering handicapped children. They knew that if Laura had survived her last apnoea attack, she would most probably have been handicapped.

'We were too young to cope with a handicapped child then,' says Pauline. 'When I was a nurse, I'd looked after a five-month-old boy in hospital with meningitis. He was left handicapped – he was deaf, blind and had fits. All the time Laura was in Special Care, I had this picture of that boy in my mind. I knew we couldn't have dealt with a child like that at the time. But a few years afterwards, we started to feel we'd been "let off", and we should give something back.'

In February 1990, Simon and Pauline were approved as foster carers for children with special needs. Five months later, their first foster-daughter, Harriet, came to live with the family. She was nine weeks old, and had profound physical and mental handicaps. She would live with them until her death two and a half years later.

Pauline says her attitude to handicap at the time Laura was born was, 'If a child's not perfect, it's not right.' 'I thought a handicapped child was a tragedy,' she says. 'And that's the attitude of most of the world – and the Church. But now I've realised that you fall in love with the child first, and the handicap afterwards. You see the child, not the handicap.'

Although Harriet was hard work, she slotted easily into the family. Mara and Thomas didn't resent her at all – rather, they were proud of her. When Thomas came home from school, he would always ask his mother, 'What sort of a day did you have – how's Harriet?' They both knew they had a 'little big sister', since their parents talked openly to them about Laura, and Pauline believes that helped them cope with Harriet.

When Harriet died, Pauline and Simon did all the things for her that they weren't able to do for Laura. The whole family – Mara and Thomas included – were with her at the end. At the back of Pauline's mind was the thought that she had deserted Laura and let her down, so when Harriet died it was Pauline who washed her, brushed her hair and carried her downstairs.

And there was a full funeral service for Harriet, too. A friend asked Pauline if she felt Harriet's funeral was replacing Laura's, as something she should have done then but was doing fifteen years later instead. But Pauline thinks not. 'They were two separate episodes,' she says. 'Yet at the same time, it was a continuation.'

After Harriet's death, the couple found it much easier to talk to other people than they had after Laura died. 'I think it's much harder to cope with the death of a baby who no one else knew,' says Pauline. 'You're very alone after the death of a neonate.

'People knew Harriet, and so we could talk about her and their memories of her. They don't get so embarrassed, and you give them the opportunity to share in the grief. With Laura, it was harder to face people in the early days, because they don't know what to talk about. They didn't know Laura, and so couldn't talk about her. In our fragile state it was hard to introduce the subject ourselves, and so it became difficult to talk to other people.'

Another difference in coping with the deaths of the two children was in their emotional reaction. 'We know God could have healed Harriet,' says Pauline. 'But through our experience with Laura, we'd learnt that healing isn't what we want it to be, but what God wants it to be. So when Harriet died, we weren't angry and depressed.

'Despite all our anger and pain when Laura died, we knew deep down that God was in control, but we just didn't "feel" that he was. It does knock your faith – but we knew there must be a purpose behind it all. Years later we can see some of that purpose, with being given the privilege of caring for Harriet.'

'You can't say the reason Laura died was so we could start fostering handicapped children,' says Simon. 'But that's been the outcome.'

On the sixteenth anniversary of Laura's death, 27 July 1994, Pauline and Simon spent some time discussing how different their lives might have been had Laura lived. Would they have changed churches? Would they have moved house? They didn't know.

'Losing Laura has made us look at life differently,' says Simon. 'It's caused us to be unsettled. Things affect us more, and we don't just accept things at face value. Life is never the same again.'

But they gain some comfort from their ability to help other couples whose babies have died – in a way that they would have appreciated help themselves.

'There was nobody to tell us what to do and what to expect – and you do need someone to guide you through those changes,' says Simon. 'We had no experience, and we were suddenly thrown into it. There's a number of people we've been able to help in that way over the years.'

'The little things count,' says Pauline. 'We would have liked people to phone us to see how things were, and just to know that people were praying. We didn't want anybody sermonising. People feel they should say something, but there's nothing they can say – it's better just to hold someone. I couldn't understand why we suffered so much when we lost Laura – but it's given us understanding for other people.

'We found out who our friends were,' she says. 'The best ones were those who made time for us, and who admitted they had no idea what we were going through but wished to help. That's how we can support other people now.'

9

Two rabbits

Alison and Richard were committed members of their lively church, leading the youth group and a homegroup. But the church was in the town centre, and they lived two miles out.

When Alison became pregnant for the second time, they were convinced that they should move nearer the church, station and major shops. They had one car, which Richard used during the week. He was a polytechnic lecturer, and Alison had been teaching until their first son, Jamie, was born in January 1977. Jamie would be twenty-two months old when their second child was due.

Although Richard and Alison searched for a suitable house, they found nothing they liked. So they decided to put an advertisement in the local paper for a four-bedroom town house. During the next two weeks, they had three replies, but all were on the wrong side of the town centre for church and parish.

One day, when Richard was walking to the church from the station, his route took him along an attractive residential road opposite a park. 'This would be nice, if it's possible,' he prayed as he walked along.

A few days later the couple received a phone call from an old lady. She told them she'd been away for some weeks, but on her return she'd looked back through the papers and seen their advertisement. She lived in a four-bedroom terraced house on the road opposite the park, and she wanted to sell. They viewed the house, which needed an enormous amount of work doing on it, but they knew it was 'the' house. They made an offer – which was accepted.

At the end of July 1978, while solicitors and building societies were doing what had to be done prior to the move, Richard and Alison took thirty teenagers from the youth group to Llangollen. Alison was exhausted. She was huge, and had difficulty walking – although the pregnancy was only halfway through. She went on most of the long walks, and did the cooking for a week, but felt this didn't explain why she was so tired – she had been so well in her first pregnancy. She assumed a second baby was always bigger than the first, and gave in to her exhaustion, collapsing into bed every evening instead of joining the young people for their evening session.

In September, the family moved house. The date of the move coincided with Alison's thirty-two-week ante-natal appointment, so she postponed it until the following week.

At her twenty-eight-week appointment, the doctors hadn't been able to work out which way up the baby was lying. At her thirty-three week appointment, Alison asked the doctor if he now knew how the baby was lying. He said he wasn't sure, and went out to fetch the registrar.

'I was lying on the bed, and Jamie, who was very articulate for twenty months, was sitting under the bed with a number book,' recalls Alison. 'He was saying, "One duck, two rabbits, three pigs," and so on. The registrar examined me, and he said, "I think we've got two rabbits in here." I was totally shocked – but thrilled and excited as well.'

Alison was sent for an X-ray – it was still pre-scan days in the old maternity hospital – and the verdict was confirmed. There were indeed two rabbits.

On the way home, crying with shock and excitement, Alison met a friend. 'She thought something awful must have happened,' says Alison, 'but when I told her, we just stood in the road, shrieking, laughing and crying all at once.'

Arriving home to a house in a state of chaos, Alison told the builder her news. Then she phoned Richard. He has a clear memory of standing by the old-fashioned photocopier in his office, picking up the phone and hearing Alison say, 'I've got news for you – it's twins!'

Richard, like Alison, was at first shocked, but excited. He told everyone at work, and anyone he met for the rest of the week.

'The joke was on us when we found we were expecting twins,' says Alison. 'We were known to be well-organised people. We'd had it all organised: we were going to have two children, with a two-year gap. I even conceived just when we planned to. But we saw the funny side – we thought it was God's sense of humour.'

The race was now on to have the house ready in time. There were only a few weeks to go, and building, rewiring and replumbing still to be done. The family was living in one room and still had no hot water.

To add to what Alison calls 'the tremendous pressure', she was told she would have to be admitted to hospital for two weeks' rest and iron injections.

At this point, the church stepped in. The move into town enabled many more people to become helpers and close friends as the 'big event' approached. Richard and Jamie were invited to a different home each day for meals; other people delivered ready-cooked meals to their door. Friends flocked in to help decorate the house, and members of the youth group arrived to clear debris and create a home.

'The whole church was excited,' remembers Alison. 'It was a thrilling time, and tremendously important in strengthening fellowship in the church. And through the whole experience, the twins being born and then Jenny dying, we learned to receive.

'We'd always been the competent, organised ones. But then we could only sit back and let the church give to us. We were on the receiving end for the first time, and we forged bonds with people which have lasted for years.'

Alison had only been out of hospital for two weeks when her labour started. The day before, she'd had an internal examination at the hospital, and had started painting in the kitchen during the evening. At one thirty the next morning, 14 November, her waters broke. Richard phoned for the ambulance, which whisked Alison off within ten minutes.

Rather than immediately phoning their friend Sue, who had arranged to stay with Jamie, Richard decided there was plenty of time – and went back to sleep. But fifteen minutes later the hospital phoned to tell him that if he wanted to see his babies born, he had better be quick. He phoned Sue, who climbed into the warm bed he had just vacated. Richard remembers Jamie telling everyone he spoke to the next day that 'Auntie Sue was in Daddy's bed this morning!'

Alison remembers a lot of laughter during the labour and birth. It was a much easier labour than her first, and she describes it as 'a lovely occasion'. Two midwives were present – one for each baby – a houseman, and the registrar. Richard found himself trapped in a corner of the small delivery room, almost unable to move!

The twins were born in less than two hours.

The couple had chosen a girl's name for their baby before they knew there were two of them: Jennifer Elizabeth. So when two little girls were born, it was very easy to name them: Jennifer *and* Elizabeth.

Elizabeth Abigail arrived first, a breech baby, who weighed seven and a half pounds. Jennifer Rachel appeared two minutes later, head down, and weighing seven pounds.

'They were both perfectly fit and healthy – and they were gorgeous,' says Richard.

They looked alike in many ways, although Libby had a rounder face and lighter skin. There was some confusion about whether they were identical or not, since the medical staff could not tell whether there was one placenta or two fused together. Richard and Alison were asked whether they would like the placenta tested, to determine whether or not the twins were identical. As it didn't matter to them either way, they decided not to have it tested. They couldn't know the significance of this decision for several months.

A week later Alison, Libby and Jenny arrived home. 'It was all very thrilling, and we thoroughly enjoyed it!' she says. 'There was a sense of involvement of the church fellowship. People would turn up, bringing meals, and do whatever jobs needed doing, or take our washing away with them.

'We had three months of total domestic activity, which was both happy and tiring,' she says. 'It was also a very busy and public three months. We were grateful for all the help, and welcomed people.

And people enjoyed being included in the happiness – in the same way as they later appreciated being included in the grief.'

Alison was breast-feeding the twins, so much of her time was taken up with them. She had to get into a careful routine, trying to balance Jamie's needs against theirs. While the girls slept, Alison felt she should have time with him.

Each day friends from church came to give general help and to bath the twins. The most difficult part of the day was the late afternoon, when Alison was feeding and Jamie was tired – so often other friends would come round specifically to play with Jamie.

'We had three babies under twenty-two months, all in nappies. My aunt bought us a tumble drier, and after the first three weeks my mum paid for me to have a cleaner,' says Alison.

The girls' personalities, responses and sleep patterns were quite different. Libby always woke first and cried loudly. She had colic. Jenny did not cry so often and rarely demanded to be fed.

Libby always woke for her feed, and Alison would wake Jenny so that both twins could be fed together. 'The image firmly fixed in my mind is of Alison sitting there with a baby at each breast,' recalls Richard. While the babies fed, Jamie would sit at a stool in front of his mother and sort buttons, draw or look at books.

The family had a special Christmas, with both sets of grandparents to stay. Richard's father was quite ill, and it was an effort for him to be there – but it turned out to be the only time he saw Jenny.

At last the family got into the routine of going out. They bought a second-hand double pram with two hoods for twenty-five pounds, and Richard adapted a seat for Jamie in the middle. Then they could occasionally go to the shops, and more regularly to church. It was winter, so they didn't go out often.

On Sunday 18 February 1979, a cold and dull day, the family set off for church. Alison had fed the twins before they went out. Jenny hadn't fed well, and had cried, which was unusual for her. But there was nothing noticeably wrong with her.

The advice given to parents then was to sleep babies on their front – unlike the advice today. Alison dressed the twins in sleeping suits with big hoods and laid them on their fronts in the pram. 'So we couldn't see their faces,' she says.

The back of the church was sectioned off for prams, and Alison left the babies asleep there. Partway through the service, Libby woke. Alison took her out of the pram, but as it wasn't time for a feed, she left Jenny to sleep.

After the service, a lady in the congregation said to Alison, 'I've never seen Jenny, she's always asleep.' Alison tried not to disturb the babies just so someone could look at them, so she smilingly said, 'No, she always sleeps better than Libby.'

Then she put Libby back in the pram, and the family went home.

As they walked down the path in the back garden, Richard and Alison saw a wren. Jenny's grandfather had nicknamed her 'Jenny Wren', and the name had stuck. They pointed it out to Jamie, and they all stopped to look at the wren as it flitted around by itself.

It was the only time – before or since – that they had seen a wren in their garden.

Alison left Libby and Jenny asleep in the kitchen while she prepared lunch. Richard has a clear memory of that lunch.

'We had lamb, followed by a rhubarb dessert – and I don't like either of them particularly. My abiding impression is of a cold, dull February day. When I think back to Christmas, my feeling is of a house that was full and warm – although it was probably just as cold and dull then. But that was my impression.'

Halfway through lunch, Libby woke for her feed. Alison picked her up, and because she fed them at the same time, she went back to get Jenny.

'Her face was down, so I couldn't see her until I picked her up,' says Alison. 'There was something wrong; she felt limp. And when I looked at her, I saw her face was squashed and blue.'

The memories of exactly what happened next are blurred and confused by the sense of panic and urgency. Richard remembers Alison yelling, and Alison recalls that her spontaneous reaction was to turn Jenny upside down and bang her on the back. Perhaps she had choked?

Jenny's colour came back. She was pink – but there was still no response, and she remained limp. Richard took over, while Alison phoned 999. She remembers shouting something like, 'Come straight away, my baby's died!'

The ambulance appeared very quickly. Somehow, either Richard or Alison had had the presence of mind to put Libby back into her coat, and Alison was rushed off to Casualty with both twins. Sue was once again summoned to fetch Jamie, and Richard chased after the ambulance in the car.

While Jenny was given oxygen in the ambulance, Libby was still crying to be fed. Arriving at the hospital, Jenny was whisked away. As Alison sat in the corridor feeding just one baby, milk was leaking out of her other breast, where Jenny would have sucked.

'I was crying out to God to help us, but even at the same time, all I could think was, "If I could feed Jenny, she'd be all right," ' says Alison. 'I kept telling the nurse that Jenny needed feeding, and the nurse was trying to tell me gently that my baby wouldn't need feeding.'

Jenny was still breathing, but the doctors told Alison and Richard that they weren't getting any brain response. 'They didn't know what was wrong with her,' says Alison, 'and they could only conclude she had something wrong with her brain, possibly a brain haemorrhage.'

The hospital rang through to the city for a paediatrician, who arrived within half an hour. He tried to find a vein to put a drip into, but Jenny's veins had collapsed. Richard remembers the young paediatrician becoming more and more upset as he searched.

All Sunday afternoon Richard and Alison waited at the hospital. They rang their parents and friends. Word shot round the church, and the desperate praying began. First the vicar arrived, then the curate. Then one of their closest friends, Hazel, who was a nurse, arrived to stay with them.

The hospital staff suggested that the vicar should ask Richard and Alison whether they wanted Jenny baptised. 'We couldn't see the point,' says Alison. 'As far as we were concerned, if she died she would go straight into the arms of Jesus, so we said it didn't matter.'

'We were quite aware she might die, but you live on two planes.

She was transferred to the Special Baby Unit, and the staff kept saying, "You do realise, don't you, that your baby is seriously ill?" '

Alison and Richard were given a room to themselves, but were able to keep going in to spend time with Jenny. She was wrapped in foil to keep her body temperature up, and was having convulsions.

'As we stood over her bed, we prayed two things,' says Alison. 'First, that if it was what God wanted, he would restore her, and she would be healed. As we prayed, her convulsions stopped, and she lay still, like her own beautiful self. We felt God met her at that point, and she was peaceful from then on.

'The second thing we prayed was more significant in the long term. We were able to say to God, "Thank you for the unexpected gift of Jenny, and thank you for the three months we have had with her. We give her back to you." That's a very important step to be allowed to take. We were given the opportunity to pray, to give her back to God, and so we never felt God had taken her from us.

'The most significant thing we started to learn that day was that our children are God's gifts, they're in his hands, and we can give them back. That applies equally to our children who are alive.'

At about six o'clock, the decision was made to take Jenny by ambulance to the city hospital, since the local staff couldn't find out what was wrong with her. But before the ambulance arrived, Jenny died. She was exactly thirteen weeks old.

The hospital staff didn't want Alison and Richard to see Jenny immediately. They asked them to wait a few minutes, and in that time, the staff washed her, dressed her in a white gown and placed a daffodil on her tummy.

When Alison and Richard saw her, there was a wry smile among the tears. The whole process of dressing her up seemed so ludicrous and irrelevant. Even the daffodil had been taken out of a bowl of half-dead flowers already in the room. But they were allowed to stay with Jenny as long as they wanted.

Then, while they rang their parents and Sue, Hazel held Libby before leaving the hospital to go to tell the church. The evening service had just started, and as soon as the congregation saw

Hazel walk to the front and hand in a note, they all knew what had happened.

Although one woman approached Hazel afterwards, expressing anger with her for disturbing the service, no one else felt like that. Years later, one friend recalls the shock, heaviness and concern among the people there. Richard and Alison's bereavement was 'a shared grief'. Stunned friends cried in each other's arms; the feeling among the congregation was that 'our baby' had died.

'We came home from the hospital to an empty house,' says Alison. 'Then one by one, those who had been at the service turned up. They just sat. People came because they wanted to come. There were no wise words, no advice, no telling us what to do. They just wanted to be with us and to cry with us. Nobody wanted to explain why it had happened, they just wanted to love us.

'Alan, the lay reader who had taken the service that evening, was never one for emotional gestures. But he was the first in the door. Libby was crying, and he took her into the kitchen to give her some colic medicine. He nursed her all evening.'

When Richard had phoned Sue from the hospital, he had asked her to take Jenny's cot away. So when they took Libby to bed, there was just one cot in the room.

At eight o'clock the coroner's officer arrived, a very gentle, semi-retired policeman, who had to get the factual information. There had been no symptoms of any illness, only the fact that Jenny hadn't fed well and had cried during her last feed.

Alison remembers the desperate need to know why – medically rather than philosophically – Jenny had died. The issue of whether there had been one or two placentas now became significant. If it wasn't known why Jenny had died, then it may have been congenital, and if the twins were identical, could Libby also die?

'We needed to know why she'd died, and we needed to know that Libby wasn't going to die too,' says Alison. The GP came to the house to examine Libby, and although he found nothing wrong, he said he would come whenever they wanted him.

It seemed an endless few days as they waited for the result of the post-mortem. They felt as though they were in limbo; they could do nothing until the result came.

When it eventually came, the cause of death was given as broncho-pneumonia. 'It was totally unexpected,' says Richard. 'We struggled to understand how or why it could have happened.'

The morning after Jenny died, a letter arrived from friends who were missionaries in Tanzania, saying their daughter Elizabeth had been born. And they later found out that another friend had a baby on the day Jenny died.

'Another thing that hit me, the day after,' remembers Richard, 'was that there were nappies to wash, and some of them were Jenny's nappies.'

In the days following Jenny's death, the church members continued to arrive at the house. 'We needed them more than ever, to just be there, not to say anything or be wise. We just talked. And they just kept coming,' says Alison.

The staff on the maternity ward where the twins spent their first week of life sent a bouquet of flowers. They had been so thrilled when the twins were born.

Alison's parents came. 'They believed, but we'd not generally talked together about our Christian faith,' she says. 'But because they were with us at that time, we just talked. We grew much closer to them in the two weeks they stayed. They went through it with us. Our friends supported them and us.'

'But even in the pain and grief there was a funny side to it,' says Alison. 'I was completely engorged with milk after feeding two babies, and I had to walk everywhere supporting my breasts. People kept wanting to hug me – and they'd get covered with milk!'

There were times, too, when they needed space. The Sunday after Jenny died, they didn't go to church, but went for a long walk instead, and then had lunch with friends.

Both Alison and Richard felt instinctively that they wanted a burial rather than a cremation. Alison feels it was because Jenny was the first person close to them to die. But when they went to see her body in the funeral parlour, they felt as if they were looking not at their daughter, but at a china doll.

'I'm so glad we went to see her,' says Alison. 'It changed how I thought. It made me realise we weren't burying our baby, and it doesn't matter what happens to the body. We felt assured of the fact that she went to be with Jesus.'

They chose words for the gravestone to reflect that assurance: 'Jennifer Rachel. 14 November 1978–18 February 1979. Jenny – With Jesus.'

They decided to have a private burial service at the cemetery with just a dozen close family and friends. Alison recalls sitting in the car, travelling to the cemetery, saying to Richard, 'I cannot believe that we are going to our daughter's burial.'

The graveyard slopes gently down to a small stream, with allotments opposite. It was a crisp, sunny day, and Richard remembers hearing the sounds of children in the playground of the local school nearby. It took just one undertaker to lift Jenny's tiny coffin from the back of the van. And her parents saw that the name had been spelt wrong on the brass plate.

'It was spelt "Jenifer",' says Alison. 'We laughed through the tears. The spelling didn't matter.'

The only request they had for the burial, which was held ten days after Jenny died, was to sing, 'Turn your eyes upon Jesus'. Then, on the Saturday, a thanksgiving service was held at the church.

'It was full,' says Alison. 'It was a shared grief with the church, and friends came from all round the country.'

Because it was not a funeral service as such, there was a chance for Richard and Alison to speak to people afterwards. Some avoided them, but most wanted to speak to them.

They were unaware of it at the time, but because they were well known at the church, they were being watched. Some of the youth group, now in their thirties, still talk of the effect it had on them. And an older couple told them later that if they had given up their faith in God, they would have done too.

'It was a good thing we didn't know about it at the time. It would have been impossible to live with,' says Alison.

Both Alison and Richard found it terribly important that they still had a baby to hold. They found that having Libby was a large part of the healing process.

Alison hasn't forgotten the physical pain in her chest, an indescribable ache. 'I would wake up feeling pain all over,' she remembers. 'It's the overwhelming thing I remember, this terrible, terrible physical pain.' She asked an elderly friend who came to visit if this dreadful hurt would ever go away, and was assured that in time, the pain wouldn't be so intense. But it was months before it went.

'Another thing that friend did was pray with me,' says Alison. 'I couldn't get rid of the picture of the horror of Jenny's face when I picked her up. It was grotesque. I'd wake up in the night and see it. My friend prayed not that this picture would go away, but that the horror would be taken from it. I wouldn't want to forget – but after she prayed, the horror had gone.'

Richard and Alison started to wonder what was in the camera. They were desperate to have photographs of Jenny – and thankfully, they had taken several pictures the day before she died. When the film was developed, the only picture that didn't come out was one of Alison breast-feeding the twins.

They didn't take photographs for months afterwards, though. There are whole chunks of Libby's development that they can't remember. They have no clear memories of Libby or Jamie in the three months after Jenny died.

After two weeks' compassionate leave, Richard returned to work.

Alison lost any confidence in her own judgement about the children's health – something which has remained with her, to a lesser degree, to the present day. If Libby seemed slightly unwell, Alison didn't trust herself to decide it was a minor ailment. It was easy to get things out of proportion, and she needed people constantly to tell her that Libby was all right. The doctor continued to visit at any time, day or night, when she called in a panic.

Her self-confidence was so weak that she stopped volunteering to babysit for other people. The responsibility of looking after babies was too great. It was not a conscious decision, and it took years for Alison to realise that was what she'd done. A hurdle was passed when friends whose house was being renovated came to live temporarily with Alison and Richard. At the beginning, Alison made sure she was never alone with their baby. But one day the mother left the house, calling out that she was going shopping for an hour, while the baby was asleep. A frightened Alison sat by the baby's cot for the whole time she was away. 'But I felt I'd achieved something,' she remembers.

During the months that followed, Alison frequently relived the whole morning of Jenny's death. 'If only I'd picked her up in church when someone wanted to see her. If I'd taken her out of the pram after we got home, it might not have happened. Should I have taken her out on such a cold day?

'I spent whole days thinking, "If we'd done this, or that . . ." Yet I knew deep down that we trusted God – despite all that was happening,' says Alison.

'Two scriptures are now engraved in us because of what happened. One is the experience of Job, at the end, where he doesn't claim to understand what had happened, but because of it, he knew God.

'We didn't understand it, and we don't now. And I don't think we have a right to understand it. But we know God better because he walked with us through the darkness.'

The other scripture which became special through Jenny's death was Psalm 139: 'Thou didst knit me together in my mother's womb . . . In thy book were written, every one of them, the days that were formed for me, when as yet there was none of them.'

'People said, "What a tragedy," ' remembers Alison. 'Yes, but I don't believe it's just that. I don't want to sound pious, but I think every day we live is planned by God.

'Neither of us has ever felt that we could blame God. And we haven't been angry. It's not that I can't have that reaction, because I *have* been angry with God when other people have died. Jenny's was a short life in our terms, but a complete one in God's terms. We know we'll meet again in heaven.'

They received many letters. The ones they found most meaningful were those that said, 'We love you, we assure you of our love, and God's love.' Those that quoted verses of scripture they just didn't take in.

'Quoting verses and expounding on them didn't help much,' says Alison. 'People do it because it helps *them*. It was the fact that people prayed for us and showed their love for us that mattered.'

Richard and Alison both wanted to see people, and they wanted to talk. They found that the sooner they saw people afterwards, the easier it was to tell them what had happened. 'The shock reaction protects you, and you're able to do things after a death that you can't do later,' says Alison. 'The longer it was after Jenny died, the more difficult it was to tell people.' About six weeks after Jenny died, Alison was pushing Libby's pram in Woolworth's, when a woman she vaguely knew asked, 'What have you done with the other twin?' Alison found it hard to tell her, and even more difficult to cope with the woman's horror at what she'd said.

Alison used to spend a lot of time visiting people living in the parish. 'I continued to visit with Jamie and Libby, and then later with Jonathan. They would want to know how we were, and let us know they cared. They didn't forget,' she says.

Jamie was only a few weeks past his second birthday when his little sister died, but he was amazingly articulate, and asked a lot of questions. Alison and Richard thought carefully about how they should explain it to him, and eventually decided to tell him that because Jenny was very poorly, Jesus had decided it would be best for her if she went to live with him.

'We believed that was the right thing to say,' Alison remembers. 'But a few days later he asked a friend if she knew when Jesus was coming to take *him* away. And if living with Jesus is so nice, why is everyone crying?'

In the three and a half years after Jenny died, the family knew a succession of deaths. Richard's father died four months after Jenny, Alison's father the following year, and her mother eighteen months later. And the church, too, was going through a difficult patch. There were five deaths in a very short time, and three of them were children.

A few months after Jenny died, Alison went to the mother and toddler group at church. She froze inside when a friend cheerfully introduced her to some new members with the words, 'This is Alison, she has two children here on earth, and one in heaven.' In her heart, Alison knew this was true – but she was unable to continue the conversation.

Two months later, that same friend's baby also died; it was a cot death. She understood, too, the pain of 'having a child in heaven'.

When the baby had been born, Alison had given him some of Jenny's clothes. When he died, she says, 'It raised enormous questions about any connection. Had he died because he wore Jenny's clothes? We had to talk about it. You're left with so many questions, and you get things out of proportion.'

The decision remained about what to do with the rest of Jenny's clothes. Many people had given the twins matching garments, and now only one set was needed. Should they give away the other set? In the end, Alison gave them to someone who had twin girls – but she didn't know the family, and passed them on through an intermediate person.

Alison had a one-time friend who had fallen out with her in the past. She struggled with the thought that, 'Maybe she's cursed us.'

'I think that reflects how vulnerable we felt at the time,' says Alison. 'We imagined all sorts of peculiar things, searching for an explanation. Have we done something to deserve this?'

Alison still finds it painful to visit the hospital where Jenny died. Just over a year later, Jamie was an in-patient in the same ward, and Alison was physically shaking while she was there. This happened again when she visited friends' children, but then the wards were changed round, which made it easier.

The couple, sometimes with Jamie and Libby, visited the grave regularly when Jenny first died. As the years went by, they didn't feel the need to go so often or to stay so long. Now, the two dates each year they feel it's important to visit the grave, taking flowers, are the anniversaries of Jenny's birth and death.

'There's a cypress tree at the end of the row of graves,' says Richard, 'and I've seen the years go by as I've watched the tree grow, and the graveyard develop.

'The cemetery is a few hundred yards from the main Euston line, and I used to go regularly to London for meetings. So I'd sit on the side of the train overlooking the graveyard, and say to myself as we passed it, "My child's buried there." '

'Little things have significance,' says Alison. 'The snowdrops were out a few days before Jenny died, and I always associate snowdrops with her.'

'And I always associate that time with smelly hyacinths and the Co-op funeral parlour,' says Richard.

Richard's experience of the years following Jenny's death, as he looks back on them, do not always parallel Alison's. 'My recollections are not as sharp and focused,' he says.

'When I look back on that time, and the years that followed, there's more of a detachment and a rolling together of events. I remember doing my research degree, my dad dying, Alison's dad dying – one memory tumbling after another. It's because we're different personalities, we respond differently. I was busy at work, and I wasn't at home all the time like Alison. Perhaps her emotional responses were deeper than mine. She could definitely articulate them better than me.'

Alison agrees, but says that although Richard was busy they were fully together in their grief. It was simply that life went on for her in one way, and for Richard in another.

'He never got impatient with me, he was always supportive and always there for me,' she says. 'He'd always pick up on how I felt when I needed him, and when I panicked.'

'Undoubtedly the experience brought us together,' says Richard. 'We trod the road together. Absolutely.'

Eventually, Alison and Richard felt they wanted another baby. Jonathan was born three and a half years after Libby and Jenny.

Alison's fear and lack of self-confidence were still with her. 'I used to prod Jonathan to make sure he was still breathing. I'd wake him up to make sure. He had a bad chest, and the doctor put him on steroids for *my* peace of mind. He didn't need them.'

She relaxed more when first Libby, and then Jonathan, reached their second birthdays, because of the link with cot death.

The couple have found that Jenny's death has become an 'event' in the life of the church. Alison likens it to the day Kennedy was killed, as people will still say, 'I remember the night Jenny died.'

But they find it strange when people ask, 'However did you get over it?'

'It's a silly expression,' says Alison. 'You don't get over it. The experience becomes part of you, and makes you become the person you are today. It changes your perception of the value of life, and makes you realise how precious every child is. It helps you empathise with what other people go through. The whole experience has changed me, knocked corners off me, made me a more gentle character.'

She laughs. 'Some people wouldn't agree with that – but they should have known me as I was before!

'God doesn't have to explain why, but he sometimes gives us experiences which soften the blow,' she goes on. 'Our relationship with my parents, and with close friends, was much deeper afterwards, because they went through it with us. We were weak and vulnerable within the church, a new experience for us – and for them, so they were able to give to our need. It bound us to all sorts of unusual people.

'If other people's faith was deepened as a result of Jenny dying, it's not a compensation or a reason, but it's a consolation. We haven't even any right to that. It's God's grace.'

Addresses of support organisations

The Compassionate Friends, 53 North Street, Bristol BS3 1EN
Tel: 01272 539639

Foundation for the Study of Infant Deaths, 5 Belgrave Square, London SW1X 8QB
Tel: 0171-235 0965

Miscarriage Association, c/o Clayton Hospital, Northgate, Wakefield, West Yorkshire WF1 3JS
Tel: 01924 200799

Stillbirth and Neonatal Death Society (SANDS), 28 Portland Place, London W1N 4DE
Tel: 0171-436 7940
Helpline: 0171-436 5881

Scottish Cot Death Trust, Royal Hospital for Sick Children, Yorkhill, Glasgow G3 8SJ
Tel: 0141-357 3946

Wholeness Through Christ, WTC Office, Waggon Road, Brightons, Falkirk, Scotland FK2 0EL

Glossary

Apgar score:
The results of quick tests carried out on a baby at one minute and five minutes old. The tests of heart rate, muscle tone, breathing, reflexes and skin colour are given scores of nought, one or two, making a total possible Apgar score of ten.

Apnoea:
A pause in breathing.

Breech:
In a breech presentation, the baby is upright in the womb, in a 'bottom down' position. This is opposite to the normal position (cephalic), in which the baby is 'head down' in the womb. It is occasionally necessary to deliver a breech baby by Caesarean section.

Caesarean section:
A surgical operation in which the baby is delivered abdominally. In some cases, the Caesarean is booked in advance; in others it is performed in an emergency, when the baby needs to be delivered quickly. Some Caesareans are done under general anaesthetic; others are carried out under epidural, in which case the mother can remain awake all the time.

D&C (Dilatation and Curettage):
A minor operation in which the cervix, or neck of the womb, is

dilated, so that the endometrium, the lining of the uterus, can be scraped. The contents of the uterus are expelled.

Epidural:
A common and effective form of pain relief, which is administered by means of a tube, through which the anaesthetic is placed in the epidural space around the spinal column. The lower half of the body is numbed completely. It can be used during vaginal delivery, or during Caesarean birth, in which case the mother can remain conscious throughout the delivery.

Gestational diabetes:
The progressive increase in insulin during pregnancy can make latent diabetes appear in certain women. This can resolve after the pregnancy.

Hydatidiform mole:
A rare and usually benign tumour which develops in early pregnancy. It affects the membrane surrounding the baby, preventing its development. Oxygen and nutrition cannot reach the baby, causing its death. If untreated, the mother may develop cancer.

Twin-to-twin transfusion:
A rare condition which can occur in identical twins, in which a connection between the placental circulations of the twins results in blood passing from one baby into the other. The baby who has received the extra blood is large, while the baby who has suffered the blood loss will be small, pale and anaemic.

IVF (In Vitro Fertilisation):
The so-called 'test-tube-baby' treatment is one of the ways in which an infertile couple can be helped to have their own child. It completely bypasses blocked Fallopian tubes in women whose ovaries are functioning normally and who have a healthy womb.

Laparoscopy:
An examination of the organs inside the abdomen, including the

reproductive organs. An illuminated laparoscope, inserted through the abdomen, allows close examination of the uterus, tubes and ovaries.

Oedema:
Swelling, which usually occurs in the hands and feet, caused by fluid retention.

Spina bifida:
A congenital abnormality of the spinal cord.